BREAD FOR
MY NEIGHBOUR

BREAD FOR MY NEIGHBOUR

AN APPRECIATION OF
THE SOCIAL ACTION AND INFLUENCE
OF WILLIAM BOOTH

by
FREDERICK COUTTS

Bread for myself is a material question:
bread for my neighbour is a spiritual question.
Nicholas Berdyaev.

HODDER AND STOUGHTON
LONDON SYDNEY AUCKLAND TORONTO

Contents

Foreword

History is unfailingly fascinating for me. It is invariably wrapped around the life of men and women who know what they want to do, and who possess the strength of character to pursue their ends with stubborn determination.

William Booth was such a man. He was convinced that he could serve God only by caring for His people and, with enormous moral courage which sprang from absolute faith in the Lord Jesus Christ, Booth persisted against formidable resistance in relating Christian belief to compassionate care for underdogs and social outcasts.

Our present welfare provisions owe more to William Booth than words can say. Inspired by the example of Christ, who would pass by none who cried out in need, he embarked on social work that was to transform the entire welfare services in this and other lands. Historians have done far less than justice to the contribution to social advance made by The Salvation Army under the leadership of William Booth. He was a spiritual giant led by God, who succeeded in awakening the conscience of Britain to the needs of people hitherto ignored.

In this book Frederick Coutts puts into proper perspective the massive social progress that has resulted from one man's life. It is a salutary reminder that there is no limit to a man's achievements when his life is completely dedicated to the service of God.

In an age when welfare benefits are looked upon as being

a natural part of civilised living, it is good for us to be reminded that progress does not come by accident. When William Booth was a babe in his mother's arms, no one could have guessed that his life would change the course of social history in so many countries. But God spoke through him as powerfully as He did through the prophets of the Old Testament.

God's power to use people has not waned. Those who, without reserve, commit themselves to His service, will find that their life is also used to advance His kingdom here 'in earth, as it is in heaven'.

Those who wear the uniform of The Salvation Army have every reason to be humbly proud of the heritage into which they have entered. Human need is still their challenge — as it is for all who seek to walk in the steps of Jesus.

This book is a forceful reminder that the only kind of life worth living is that which is inspired by the love of Christ. I hope that young people who read this fantastic story will be led to give their life to the Lord Jesus and say: 'Here am I, send me.'

George Thomas.

A Salvation Army home for destitute men was recently opened in an African capital. 'I like it very much,' said one new arrival approvingly, 'for it has prayers *and* hot water.'

1

What Doth the Lord Require?

In his introduction to the English edition of *Socialism:
Utopian and Scientific*, published in 1892, Friedrich Engels
wrote that The Salvation Army 'revives the propaganda of
early Christianity, appeals to the poor as the elect, fights
capitalism in a religious way, and thus fosters an element of
early Christian class antagonism.' The first phrase is true;
the second a half-truth; the third and fourth false.

Engels was not the first, nor has he been the last, to pass
such a confusion of truth and error as a considered judgment upon the work of William Booth. This is the reason for
this attempt to reassess his influence upon the eighty years
which lie between the introduction of the Poor Law Amendment Act of 1834 and the passing of the National Insurance
Act of 1911. This period virtually coincides with his life and
death. Booth was a boy of five when elected Boards of
Guardians with paid full-time officials were introduced to
administer the Poor Law, and he lived to hear the thirty-two
year old Winston Churchill announce that a line should be
drawn 'below which we will not allow persons to live and
labour.'

A survey of this kind demands the detailed expertise of a
professional sociologist — which this writer is not — but a
lifetime of service as an officer of The Salvation Army has
given him some knowledge of the work and influence of
William Booth apparently not enjoyed by all students of the
social scene. How else can be explained the uneven treatment meted out to one of the most compassionately practical
spirits of the nineteenth century who, whatever his mistakes,

was never on the make for himself? Or the cursory dismissal of his efforts to grapple with what Alexis de Tocqueville called England's deepest trouble — the condition of the poor? Or the bland omission of his name from the Victorian record altogether?

One school of thought passes him by because he was unashamedly religious. One so avowedly bent on preparing his fellows for the life to come could have had little of value to say about the life that now is. Using a limited number of highly selective quotations from his public utterances, it is possible to argue such a case. Admittedly those who regard the Christian faith as a hindrance rather than a help to social progress, and believe that man is capable of working out his own salvation, will have little time for one who began his public life as a youthful street corner evangelist. He can be ignored without loss.

This is the offhand treatment given him in such a standard work as the marvellously detailed and informative *The Common People, 1746–1946* by G. D. H. Cole and Raymond Postgate, (Methuen, 1961 ed.). Charles Booth is properly given his due place, but the only other Booth to be named is an H. J. W. Booth, *agent provocateur*, concerned in 1917 with the prosecution of a middle-aged lady, her two daughters and son-in-law who lived in Derby. *In Darkest England and the Way Out* is listed under 'Wages and conditions' in the bibliography, but the entry given in the list of important dates for the commencement of the work of The Salvation Army is inaccurate. 1880 is meaningless. William Booth began in the East End of London in 1865; the title — 'The Salvation Army' — was first used in 1878; *In Darkest England* was published in 1890.

There is also a single phrase of ten words which declares that 'The Salvation Army sent the profits on *The War Cry* to the strike funds of the London dockers in the autumn of 1889.' This also is an error, but one which unfortunately is repeated in Norman and Jeanne Mackenzie's recent study — *The First Fabians* (Weidenfeld & Nicolson, 1977).

What actually happened was that William Booth opened a subscription fund to provide meals for the strikers and their families. The first list of donations appeared in *The War Cry* for September 7th, 1889, and continued weekly until the end of the month, by which time £543. 1s. 3d. had been raised in sums ranging from 2d. to £50. In addition, The Salvation Army in Australia cabled William Booth to draw on their own territorial funds up to £200. This enabled an average of seven thousand meals to be served daily for the duration of the strike from the Army's food distribution centre in the West India Dock Road. A half-penny fed a hungry adult: a farthing a starving child; and of this work *The Times* wrote:

> The Salvation Army is continuing to do a vast amount of good at their depot in the West India Dock Road, and it is the opinion of the leaders of the strike that had it not been for this piece of relief work the distress would have been much greater. On Saturday, 8,188 meals were served to the destitute ... The large hall was filled with children, all of whom presented a most destitute and emaciated appearance. These having been given a good meal were sent away, and the women were afterwards admitted and fed.

Later in the month a special correspondent of *The Daily News* reported in fuller detail:

> For a long time before the strike it was known that The Salvation Army had been giving food and shelter at very low rates ... But the sudden cutting off of wages soon reduced a large proportion of the dock labourers to a point of destitution at which ... even half-penny basins of soup were unattainable luxuries ... (whereupon) Mr. Booth determined to issue food tickets at half the previous prices ...
>
> Day after day throngs of famishing men, women and children crowded in with their penny paper tickets which

had been issued to the Strike Committee in rolls of 240 for ten shillings. Between Sunday morning and Wednesday night 22,000 of these tickets were presented, and twenty men have been constantly employed in preparing and dealing out halfpenny and farthing meals . . .

After this work had been going on for some time another centre was deemed desirable, and the barracks in Whitechapel Road was turned over to food supply. This was opened last Wednesday week and by Sunday afternoon — the Army has kept its food sales going on Sundays as well as weekdays — 14,558 people have been fed . . .

Cole and Postgate rightly associate the name of Cardinal Manning with the dockers' struggle, but that of William Booth is not mentioned.

Other social studies make equally brief comment. For example, in *The Victorians* (C.U.P., 1966), Joan Evans discerningly describes the Army as making 'human happiness, if only among the dregs of society, a factor in the ethics of religion', and compares Dr. Pusey quoting the opinion of St. Basil that a man must never marry his deceased wife's sister with William Booth spending 'his time thinking out how the output of empty tins from urban households can be employed for the good of the poor.'

Janet Roebuck is more abrupt. In her *The making of modern English society from 1850*, (Routledge and Kegan Paul, 1973), justice is deemed to be done in a dozen words. About half-way through, in a description of the widespread disillusionment which assailed Great Britain in the inter-war period, there is a single sentence to the effect that 'some vigorous religious groups, such as The Salvation Army, attracted new recruits.'

At least the statement is accurate — but what is to be made of the relevant paragraph in the *Outline and guide to the main social and economic questions of the second half of the nineteenth century*, prepared by J. J. N. McGurk and

published in 1966 by Allman and Son as revision notes for
'A' level social history, 1850–1900? This reads:

> In Nonconformity there were many social reforming
> elements ... but by far the greatest branch of Methodism
> was The Salvation Army, which concentrated on relief
> for the poor. General Booth ... believed that the divisions
> in society made it impossible for the envoys of the rich to
> reach the masses for the cause of Christ. The Army was
> founded on the conviction that the poor could be made
> Christian only by people of their own class. The Salvation-
> ists had no particular doctrines; they accepted what was
> accepted by all orthodox people of God.

This — 'confusion' is not too strong a word — may be
the reason why other writers deem silence to be golden. The
blurb on the back cover of *England in the Nineteenth Century*
(Pelican) describes the theme of the book as 'the major
social changes which the people of England experienced between the battle of Waterloo and the first world war', but
nowhere does William Booth appear. Gillian Avery's *Victorian People* (Collins, 1970) and Richard Altick's *Victorian
People and Ideas*, (J. M. Dent, 1973), are similarly silent.

The opposite approach is to give William Booth and the
Movement which he founded the full treatment — as is done
in *Patterns of Sectarianism*, edited by Bryan Wilson,
(Heinemann, 1967), which announces that here 'a great
many of the data are given scholarly presentations for the
first time'.

The reader is thus prepared for the array of footnotes to
be found on all but the last of the nearly sixty pages devoted
to The Salvation Army. But the first footnote on the first
page of this study (p. 49) reveals a confusion between Booth
father and Booth eldest son. Bramwell attended the corona-
tion of Edward VII in 1902; it was William who was received
at Buckingham Palace in 1904. Nor did (as the same footnote states) the St. Paul's service in 1944 mark the centenary

of William Booth's birth — which was in 1829 — but of his conversion. Nor was George Scott Railton 'the (Army's) first Chief of Staff' (p. 75n.). Railton was General Secretary of The Christian Mission from 1873 until, at his own request, he led the pioneer party of Salvationists to the United States in 1880. The title 'Chief of the Staff' was first applied to Bramwell Booth in January, 1881.

But enough; our rank structure is without doubt as perplexing as that of any other ecclesiastical hierarchy, and one feels a good deal of sympathy for the writer who, in his final sentence, confesses to 'the complexities involved in any sociological analysis of The Salvation Army'. But might not his real difficulty be that he is simply using the wrong set of tools? Does it lighten anyone's darkness to quote Weber's dictum that 'The Salvation Army was an important example of that type of religious orientation which is characterised by "soteriological orgies or other such phenomena" — these constituting functional equivalents of magical rituals for the alleviation of suffering and deprivation'? Or earlier to declare that the Army bore 'some manifestations of a value-oriented movement — in its concern with the reconstruction of older societal values, such as a patriarchal family system, behaviour patterns congruent with a rural way of life and, most comprehensively, what was in effect a feudal conception of the social structure'? But surely the compass is well and truly boxed when the last line but one of this scholarly study deems it 'appropriate to regard the Movement ... in some respects (as) an order within Anglicanism'!

Again, other judges hold William Booth's academic limitations against him. 'How knoweth this man letters, having never learned?' A boy who left school at the age of thirteen to begin a six year apprenticeship to a pawnbroker in the Goosegate, Nottingham, is hardly the stuff of which Ph.D.'s are made. If that is the charge Booth could well plead that twelve months' unemployment in the hungry forties furnished him with a more thorough-going education in the facts of life than many an armchair reformer ever received. Is there not a faint smell of intellectual snobbery when the title of 'General' is carefully placed within inverted commas four times over — as happens in Maurice Bruce's *The Coming of the Welfare State* (Batsford, 1961)? Is it really necessary to be 'plus royaliste que le roi'? Queen Victoria addressed William Booth as General as far back as 1897. Even that stronghold of social conservatism, the British War Office, recognised Salvation Army titles early in 1905. And along with this goes a slight but discernible reluctance to give William Booth credit where credit is due.

For instance, in the above-mentioned study the chapter on unemployment in the section headed 'The turning point' refers to a proposal by Canon Barnett for 'the establishment of farm colonies in the country to which unemployed men might be sent for work ... while their families were supported at home'. Eight lines lower down on page 160 is a disconnected statement that 'The Salvation Army had for some years supported a farm colony.' But nowhere is it said that at the beginning of 1904 the Hadleigh Colony had announced their continued willingness to negotiate with local government bodies for the reception of able-bodied destitute men on conditions to be mutually agreed.

Or that on May 10th of the same year George Lansbury wrote to the *Essex Weekly News* approving the work at Hadleigh in general, and in particular the treatment of a group of men sent by the Poplar Board of Guardians to Hadleigh during the previous winter for a period of six months at a capitation grant of ten shillings per week.

Or that in the autumn of the same year the Mansion House Committee — on which Canon Barnett served — announced that, so far as the previous winter's experience was concerned, 'there was a most marked change in the physical condition of the men towards the end of their stay (at Hadleigh): the regular diet, fresh air and outdoor employment have improved the health of all of them, and made them into strong, robust men.'

Of course there are a number of assessments which are objective beyond reproach. They allow the facts to speak for themselves — as do Royston Pike's *Human documents of the age of the Forsytes* (Allen and Unwin, 1969), the two volumes of *Contemporary Sources and Opinions in British History* (Warne & Co., 1967) and P. J. Keating's latest paperback — *Into Unknown England* (Fontana) — though on this see below. The specialised study by Alison Plowden of the raising of the age of consent entitled *The Case of Eliza Armstrong* (B.B.C., 1974) and Ann Stafford's *The Age of Consent* (Hodder and Stoughton, 1964) also merit the highest praise.

The one serious misinterpretation which calls for correction is that which presents William Booth as trying to shore up his failing evangelical efforts by what is now called community service. Somewhere about 1890 — take a year or two either way, so runs the argument — he came to the conclusion that 'social reform (was) an essential prerequisite to the saving of souls.' The operative word is 'prerequisite' — as though the Movement which, under God, he had founded in 1865 and which by this time had spread to all five continents, was sinking into sorry ineffectiveness.

To be fair to Peter Keating, the line taken in his earlier study — *Fact and fiction in the East End* in the second of the two encyclopedic volumes entitled *The Victorian City*, edited by Dyos and Wolff (Routledge and Kegan Paul, 1973) — is subtly modified in his introduction to the more than thirty pages of extracts from *In Darkest England and the Way Out* which appear in *Into Unknown England*. But it must also be said that the substance of this misinterpretation is repeated in the general preface which refers to 'Booth's recognition that The Salvation Army could not hope to succeed in its spiritual work unless it first concentrated on the curing of social ills.' It is the word 'first' which cannot be justified.

As with any other man of open mind William Booth had doubtless known a conflict of ideas as to the cause and cure of poverty. He had witnessed at close quarters its harsh influence upon the lives of others. He had experienced its bitterness himself. He doubtless had more than one change of mind how best to tackle this complaint. But that he suddenly bethought himself of social service as a gimmick wherewith to restore his ineffective evangelical enterprises is a travesty of his thought and action.

It can be argued that on this relationship between men's spiritual and social needs he was not wholly consistent. What matter? As with every other pioneer, he proceeded by trial and error. He learned from experience. Like his contemporary, Walt Whitman, he could have said: 'Do I contradict myself? Very well, I contradict myself.' But he never followed the practice of others of his day in accepting the condition of the poor as divinely ordained, from which state they could no more be protected than from the east wind. 'There may be', he once said to his officers at a social conference, 'a godly poverty which is hallowed by God's presence, but that is not to say that God approves destitution.'

Nor did William Booth. A contemporary drawing of the People's Mission Hall in Whitechapel which he acquired in 1869 shows a mid-day religious meeting in progress under the front porch of one part of the building, while the adjacent section carries the legend 'People's soup and coffee house', with a sign overhead in equally bold lettering: 'Australian sheep tongues — 1d.; ready cooked — 1½'. Any who wish to call this crude can do so, but in fact it is a real life illustration of the truth of Bishop Westcott's saying that there is nothing secular save that which is sinful. Here was a nineteenth-century transcription of our Lord's words about the cup of cold water given in His name.

G. M. Trevelyan set the issue fairly in his *English Social History* when he wrote that 'The Salvation Army regarded social work and care for the material conditions of the poor and outcast as being an essential part of the Christian mission to the souls of men and women.' Elie Halevy said much the same in his *Imperialism and the Rise of Labour* (Benn, 1929) when he defined the Army as 'a corps of missionaries who ... opened their preaching halls — their Forts — to all indiscriminately ... They reproached English Puritanism with its middle class respectability and a culpable failure to understand that a man of the lower classes was inevitably blinded to religion by the conditions of his lot. His spiritual and bodily welfare could not be separated.'

To William Booth and his soldiers the work of redemption embraced the whole man. He himself never claimed to be an academic economist or sociologist. He was first and last an evangelist, but never an evangelist who was content to preach sermons and then count the heads of kneeling penitents. He understood the biblical word salvation as bringing health — physical, mental and spiritual — to every man. In this respect he was of the honourable order of our own sixteenth-century Hugh Latimer, evangelist, bishop and martyr, who proclaimed the need for a personal Christian experience which would be expressed in a lively concern for one's neighbour.

The lineage of the first Salvationist was more ancient still, dating back to the Hebrew prophet of the sixth century before Christ, to whom the word of the Lord came, saying:

> Is not this what I require of you as a fast:
>   to loose the fetters of injustice,
>   to untie the knots of the yoke,
>   to snap every yoke
>   and set free those who have been crushed?

> Is it not sharing your food with the hungry,
>   taking the homeless poor into your house,
>   clothing the naked when you meet them,
>   and never evading a duty to your kinsfolk?
>   (Isaiah 58: 6–8, N.E.B.)

No radical is more true to his name than the biblical radical who sees that the salvation of society must include the salvation of the individual, and that the one will never be completely accomplished without the other. No genuine radical will turn a blind eye to the obstinate fact of human egoism, supposing that it will go away because he chooses not to notice it. What he is facing is that surd in human nature which puts paid to the vain dream of a Christian order of society without the practice of Christian grace. No mere rearrangement of the household furniture is by itself a recipe for a happy home. That all depends upon the people who live there. Norman Angell hit the right nail on the head when he said to *The Social Gazette*: 'I have always urged that our real enemies are not one another — our common enemies are error, passion, ignorance. The Salvation Army is fighting the real enemy.'

2

The Affliction of My People

It was a blessing in disguise for William Booth that he was
not born with a silver spoon in his mouth, for this meant that
he became one of that elect company of religious and social
reformers in nineteenth-century England who personally
experienced the poverty which he sought to alleviate.
Samuel Barnett might ask for a parish in Whitechapel,
Charles Booth dedicate himself to painstaking research into
the 'Life and labour of the poor in London', the seventh
Earl of Shaftesbury champion a legion of good causes —
but these worked from the vantage point of their own secure
position in Victorian society. William Booth knew what it
was to suffer the final ignominy — that of being unemployed
himself. He actually sat where the poor sat. Fellow feeling
made him wondrous kind.

He was born on April 10th, 1829, at 12 Notintone Place,
Sneinton, Nottingham, the second son of the five children
of Samuel Booth by Mary Moss, his second wife. Samuel
was an unsuccessful speculative builder and, when William
was thirteen years of age, withdrew him from school in order
to apprentice him to a Francis Eames whose pawnbroking
business was on the corner of Goosegate and Mill Alley.
Five months later, Samuel died, leaving no assets of any
consequence, whereupon the widow and her four surviving
children moved to what is thought to have been Holland
(now Brightmoor) Street, where she maintained a precarious
livelihood by the sale of needles and cottons, threads and
wools. William's weekly wage of six shillings was now the
family's one stable income — if only because the pawn-

broking business was as established a feature of urban life as the publican's.

No shop was better patronised. Literally millions of articles were pawned and repawned in the larger cities and towns of the United Kingdom in the course of a year. The usual pledge was no more than a shilling or two and, after the Act of 1872, the pawnbroker was limited to a charge of one halfpenny on every two shillings loaned for a period not exceeding one month. This seemingly trivial rate concealed an annual interest charge of 25 per cent — but needs must where the devil drove. One Nottingham mayor of this period declared that sheer destitution drove many of the poor to pawn every article of worth which they possessed, and their plight was mourned in one of the many street ballads of the day.

> They've bated our wages so low for our work
> That to gain half maintenance we slave like a Turk;
> When we ask for our money comes paper and string,
> Dear beef and bad mutton or some suchlike thing.
> Good people, O pity our terrible case,
> Pray take no offence though we visit this place;
> We crave your assistance and pray for our foes,
> O may they find mercy when this life we lose.

Booth's five years' apprenticeship was to confront him with a poverty which enfeebled a man's body and bruised his soul. No English industrial town was a paradise in the mid-nineteenth-century — Nottingham less than most. His family was now part of a population of some 50,000 people, living within a constricted area less than two miles in circumference. On two sides the town was hemmed in by lordly estates whose boundaries were inviolable. On the other two were the Lammas fields, covering some eight hundred acres, over which the freemen of the borough possessed certain rights of pasture. As these also afforded opportunities for recreation to old and young alike, any encroachment upon them was stoutly resisted by both freemen and the corporation, and not until the Inclosure Act of 1845 was this stranglehold broken.

Held in this vice Nottingham earned the unenviable reputation of being 'the unhealthiest and most overcrowded town in England.' Into this severely limited space were packed eleven thousand dwellings, seven thousand of which — reported the 1844 Health of Towns Commission — were built not only back to back but side to side. Many of these were arranged in narrow courts entered by tunnels about a yard wide, eight feet high and upwards of thirty feet long. At one end were the common privies which were not cleared until their contents had overflowed, and this highly-prized natural product was then dumped in the streets to be sold to farmers. Removal was supposed to be under cover of darkness, so that it was not surprising that the carts frequently allowed part of their semi-fluid load to spill over on to the highway. Equally not surprising that twice in William Booth's boyhood cholera broke out in the town. Nottingham was one of the ten towns in England and Wales with the highest mortality rate due to diarrhoeal diseases. Disraeli's description of Wodgate where —

at every fourth or fifth house, alleys seldom a yard wide, and streaming with filth, opened out on to the streets ... while from the principal courts often branched out a number of smaller alleys, or rather narrow passages, than which nothing can be conceived more squalid and obscure —

could have been written of Nottingham.

The main industry in the town was hosiery knitting and, behind the long garret windows of the knitters' cottages, the very old and the very young joined forces. 'As poor as a stockinger' had been a proverb for the better part of a century, for the average adult wage was seven shillings a week, and to earn that the whole family had to play its part.

'It is common,' declared one of the many commissions of the time, 'to find fifteen to twenty children in a low garret, twelve feet square, working for fifteen hours a day.'

These were facts Booth never forgot. 'When but a mere child,' he wrote in the second paragraph of his preface to *In Darkest England and the Way Out*, 'the degradation and helpless misery of the poor stockingers of my native town, wandering gaunt and hunger stricken through the streets droning out their melancholy ditties ... kindled in my heart yearnings to help the poor which have continued to this day.' This was no extravagance of phrase. The best remembered of the disjointed recollections of his early manhood to be embodied in the opening chapters of his official biography have to do with the sights and sounds of small children crying for bread in the streets of Nottingham.

The second major experience of his adolescence was his introduction to the politics of contention. Harold Begbie quotes W. T. Stead as saying that William Booth 'grew up in an atmosphere of unrest, in a hot-bed of quasi-revolutionary discontent.'

The Reform Act of 1832 still left two out of every three adult males without the vote. Chartism was born of the demand of the London Working Men's Association for universal manhood suffrage, voting by ballot, annual parliaments, equal electoral districts, payment of members and the removal of any property qualification from candidates for election. But Chartism was also a bread and butter question. 'Famishing men cannot wait,' said General Sir Charles Napier from his headquarters in the Wheeler Gate from which he commanded the Northern Division of the Army. While he was in charge there was not only order in Nottingham but peace as well. 'Thank God not a drop of blood spilled,' he wrote.

Unhappily for the town, Napier was appointed to India and in the summer of 1842 there was a by-election when the Quaker, Joseph Sturge, who was supported by the Chartists, was opposed by John Walter, editor of *The Times*. Sturge refused to resort to bribery. Walter practised it so brazenly that he was subsequently unseated. Sturge could well have prayed to be delivered from his friends, for he had the doubtful blessing of the support of Feargus O'Connor, who, having completed a prison sentence for sedition, seized the leadership of a movement which he had not created.

A few weeks after the election, an early morning strike meeting was twice broken up by the authorities, whereupon a call went out for all factories to cease working. Thousands of men massed on the Mapperly Hills. Their intentions were doubtless as varied as their plans were uncertain — but four hundred were arrested. Booth was still in his early teens but, wrote Begbie, 'in all the thousands no more enthusiastic disciple than he ... He went to the (Chartist) meetings, cheered their speakers, and subscribed to the Charter ... "The Chartists are for the poor," the boy reasoned, "therefore I am for the Chartists." '

As with more than one working-class movement, the leader failed the led. O'Connor's 'active but ill-regulated brain' — the phrase is the Hammonds' in *The Age of the Chartists* — was his worst enemy. He could brook no rival near him and so antagonised those who might have aided him. He appealed to force while unwilling to recognise the inevitable cost of force. He aroused emotions in his mainly illiterate followers which he could not satisfy, though for a brief hour he frightened the country. Two days before the Chartists descended on London for their national rally on Kennington Common on April 10th, 1848, the Queen left for Osborne. Wellington garrisoned the Bank of England, barricaded the Thames bridges, and lined the banks of the river from Waterloo to Millbank with artillery. Charles Kingsley has described how, on Waterloo Bridge, he passed the rain sodden remnants of the rally returning home, and public dread of the Chartists changed to public derision. Four years later O'Connor was declared insane. Nevertheless the defeated were the ultimate victors. Five of their six claims have since been secured.

The youthful William Booth had a third discovery to make — that of man's spiritual needs, including his own.

He had begun by attending the Church of England where he had been christened but, after his father's death, commenced to frequent the Wesley Chapel in Broad Street. Here he joined a class meeting; was present at revival gatherings conducted by Isaac Marsden and James Caughey and, happily for himself, found a good friend in a slightly older lad, William Sansom. Latterly he had never been wholly at ease on these church occasions. What was troubling him at heart was a trivial trading affair which he had undertaken on behalf of some of his companions who had rewarded him with a silver pencil case, unaware that he had made a profit for himself on the side. This concealment was more than his youthful conscience could bear. He sought the quiet of one of the class rooms in the chapel basement, and rose from his knees to seek out the lad whom he felt he had deceived. This done, a burden was lifted such as fell from Christian's back at the sight of the Cross. It may seem a far cry from the excitement born of the torrid oratory of a Feargus O'Connor to this solitary and inward decision, but this act was the source of the motivation which was to sustain him for the rest of his days. Now there was nothing in his life to hinder his total dedication to God for the service of man.

The shape of things to come was to be discerned in the next few months. The twelve-hour day at the Goosegate pawnshop had still to be served, but thereafter the freedom of the narrow Nottingham streets gave Booth and Sansom their heaven-sent opportunities for open-air preaching. At first the younger lad was unwilling either to preach or to pray publicly, but once he had brought himself to mount the borrowed chair which served as rostrum, he became the recognised leader of the group. The outdoor gathering would conclude with an invitation to any interested listener to join in the informal meetings which would be held in one of the nearby cottages. In such a fashion Booth preached his first sermon in a room which opened directly on to Kid Street. An upturned box served as a reading desk; a candle on either side of an open Bible gave light; the unlettered congregation filled the small room and clustered outside on the pavement.

By now William Booth had recognised that man was no disembodied spirit. Brother body needed food as well as brother soul. His own encounters with poverty but confirmed what the Scriptures taught that —

> if a brother or sister be naked, and destitute of daily food, and one of you say unto them, Depart in peace, be ye warmed and filled; notwithstanding ye give them not those things which are needful to the body; what doth it profit?

One day the two lads came across a homeless alcoholic lying in the street. Booth felt he could not leave her there, common sight though this was. Sansom was not so sure. Drunks were drunks, and a drunken woman could go on drinking herself into the grave. But he was overruled by his companion who spoke of finding the woman a room, providing her with a few sticks of furniture, not forgetting some decent used clothing as well. The pawnshop had taught Booth that some worn articles could be almost as good as new. Not sudden in a minute was all accomplished, but in due season Sarah was fed, clothed, housed — and converted. Theologically illiterate she might be, but she was saved.

Much the same happened with another local reprobate, Besom Jack, who subsequently became the faithful devotee of the two young evangelists. Booth went on to create a minor sensation in Wesley Chapel when he marched through the front door a motley crowd of lads and girls who had been in the habit of whiling away their time on Sundays in The Meadows — a stretch of open fields near to the Trent Bridge cricket ground. A conference was hastily convened as soon as the service was over. The minister and stewards were too good Wesleyans to wish to bar anyone from their services. Had not Charles himself written, and had they not themselves sung:

> Come, sinners, to the gospel feast,
> Let every soul be Jesus' guest;
> Ye need not one be left behind,
> For God hath bidden all mankind.

Nevertheless, future visitors of this kind were to use a side entrance and to sit where they could hear yet not be seen.

Booth was to face harsher problems of his own before long. His apprenticeship concluded, his employment ended. Francis Eames pleaded that the business could not afford a man's wage. Booth was out of work for a year. 'Those twelve months,' he said afterwards, 'were among the most desolate in my life. You may say, where was the church to which I belonged? Where were its rich members who might surely have found employment for one who was already showing promise of a useful life? It was a question we asked — for no one took the slightest interest in me.'

The eldest girl of the family had already left for London and, having married, sent home glowing reports of how she was faring. William resolved to go to London as well, but all he could find was a living-in position in another pawnbroker's shop at 1, Kennington Row, Kennington Common. But before long the lad was befriended by a South London boot manufacturer who, impressed by his pulpit abilities, suggested that he gave up pawnbroking and devoted himself to the work of an evangelist. How much a week could he live on? Frugal as ever, Booth calculated that he could manage on twelve shillings weekly. This was to improve on Bob Cratchit who was paid fifteen shillings a week — though on that he could not afford an overcoat. However, Booth was offered twenty shillings a week for three months, and on this rented two rooms at five shillings a week with a widow woman at 11 Princes Row, near Camberwell Gate.

His new-found benefactor did him a far, far greater service by encouraging his friendship with Catherine Mumford, recently arrived in Brixton from Ashbourne (Derbyshire) via Boston. Nearly one hundred pages of the Hodder & Stoughton paperback, *Catherine Booth*, by Commissioner Catherine Bramwell-Booth, are devoted to an account of their mutual affection which embraced body, mind and soul.

Catherine supported her husband-to-be through his early hesitant choices and then — married on June 16th, 1855, when both were twenty-six years of age — supported him in his regular ministry in the Methodist New Connexion.

Supported him at the decisive Liverpool Conference of 1861 which ruled that he should continue in circuit work and refused to release him for full-time evangelism.

Supported him in his resignation though it left her without home and regular income, and supported him amid the vicissitudes of the four years of itinerant evangelism which followed.

Supported him while bearing eight children — Bramwell (March 8th, 1856), Ballington (July 28th, 1857), Catherine (September 18th, 1858), Emma (January 8th, 1860), Herbert (August 26th, 1862), Marian (May 4th, 1864), Evangeline (December 25th, 1865) and Lucy (April 28th, 1868) — and went on supporting him when he declared that he had found his destiny — in the East End of London. None but a man in whom there was no guile would have announced that the Whitechapel Road led to his promised land. And none but a women of equal sincerity would have replied: 'Well, if you feel you ought to stay, stay!'

3

Execute True Judgment

What then was this parish which William Booth elected to make his own?

It was virtually an unknown land though he had visited one small part of it ten years earlier. 'Felt much sympathy for the poor, neglected inhabitants of Wapping,' he wrote in his diary, 'as I walked down their filthy streets.' Otherwise London — and particularly East London — was darkest London to him. And dark to the general public as well. 'We are not accustomed to take travellers to the East End,' said the Cheapside branch of Messrs. Thomas Cook & Son to Jack London at the beginning of the present century. 'We receive no call to take them there, and we know nothing about the place at all.'

If Victorian London was then the largest city in the world, twice the size of Paris, the East End — and the name did not come into general use until the eighties — was a city on its own, greater than Berlin, and separated from the rest of the metropolis by a wall of poverty so intimidating that it needed no manning by frontier guards. Mayhew described himself as 'a traveller in the undiscovered country of the poor'. G. R. Sims did not publish his account of *How the Poor Live* until 1883, nor was 'The bitter cry of outcast London' heard until the same year. The first of Charles Booth's seventeen volumes of *Life and Labour of the People of London* did not appear until 1889. William Booth's *In Darkest England and the Way Out* followed a year later, but the twentieth century had begun before C. F. G. Masterman wrote anonymously *From the Abyss*, which the American

Jack London followed up by describing his seven weeks'
experience in the East End under the title of *The People of
the Abyss*.

These were widely read as a species of travellers' tales.
Were those who lived east of Aldgate Pump really human?
This was what Rosa Dartle wanted to know. 'Are they
animals or clods or beings of another order?' — and Steer-
forth's answer applied to more than Peggotty and his
relations who were the immediate cause of the question.

'Why, there's a pretty wide separation between them and
us,' he replied with indifference. 'They are not expected to
be as sensitive as we are. Their delicacy is not to be shocked
or hurt very easily ... They have not very fine natures, and
they may be thankful that, like their coarse rough skins,
they are not easily wounded.'

'Really,' said Miss Dartle. 'Well, I don't know, now, when
I have been better pleased than to hear that.'

Her view was widely shared. When the young Prince
Albert asked Palmerston what the peasants were called in
England, the reply was 'Clods'. Frederick Denison who, to
his credit, lived for eight months in Stepney after graduating
at Oxford, described the shoppers in Petticoat Lane as a
'trembling mass of maggots in a lump of carrion.' Perhaps
he had been too much influenced by Matthew Arnold who,
from the same city of dreaming spires, referred to 'these
vast, miserable, unmanageable masses of sunken people.'
Carlyle wrote of the division into 'dandies and drudges' a
decade before Disraeli coined the phrase 'the two nations,'
between whom there was 'no intercourse and no sympathy.'

Because of this even much well-intentioned charity was
offered *de haut en bas*. 'Thank you, your leddyship,' ran the
script under a cartoon of an unemployed labourer's wife
receiving an alms. 'God bless you; we shall meet again in
Heaven.' 'Goodness gracious, I hope not,' was the tart reply.

If the existence of 'the raw and blind masses' could not be
denied, this was not to allow their claim upon public sympathy. To be poor was their due station in life. It was God

who had made men high and lowly. Poverty was a permanent feature of society. The Scriptures could be quoted in support of that fact. The two nations drifted further and further apart. 'Respectability and culture have fled. The lowest sets the tone of East End existence,' said Beatrice Potter. 'The altered condition of the district,' explained a Victorian Methodist weekly, 'the extension of the suburbs, the ready means of travel, have led the prosperous to migrate, and the consequence is that (the chapels at) Spitalfields, St. George's, the Seamen's Grove Road, and Brunswick, Limehouse, have emptied.'

It was enough to reduce any Christian soul to despair. Here were circumstances, declared Mark Rutherford — and William Hale White (his proper name) was no older than William Booth — which 'neither a Jesus nor a Paul could have overcome . . . In fact, no known stimulus, nothing ever held up before men to stir the soul into activity, can do anything so long as our backstreets are the cesspools they are now.'

Into this slough of despond William Booth deliberately plunged — not to prepare a thesis about low income groups in Bethnal Green. Details of that kind of economic analysis he borrowed, with due acknowledgment, from Charles Booth. He accepted his namesake's figure that about a million inhabitants of London were dependent on a family income of 20s. a week or less. Nor did he turn the distress of his fellows into his own gain by writing a book about their plight which would add to his personal income. The profit of £7,383 on *In Darkest England and the Way Out* was handed over to that scheme intact. Not that he had any instant remedy for the sheer physical want of the East End. Even had he possessed such a blue print he lacked the resources to implement it. But he had sufficient faith in God — this basic fact cannot be ignored — not to despise the day of small things.

In the year before his death he confessed to an international conference of his social officers that 'for a long time' he had been unable clearly to see how to fulfil 'the commands of my Lord, who had expressly told me that I was to feed the hungry, clothe the naked, care for the sick and visit the prisoner.' But the fact that he could not see the end from the beginning did not prevent him beginning. The report published two years and two months after he had taken charge of the tent mission in Thomas (now Vallance) Street, Whitechapel, showed how he made such a start. Four main activities were listed, the second of which had to do with the General Poor Fund. 'With this,' he explained, 'we help the poor indiscriminately, that is, without regard to whether they belong to the Mission or not, the only condition being want. Inquiry as to need is always made before help is given.'

Want abounded because the economic situation was worsening. Shipbuilding in the Poplar yards collapsed between 1866 and 1868. A bad harvest was followed by a harsh winter. By the end of the year Booth was writing: 'Only the government can give effectual assistance, but it is to be feared that, in the coming short session, too many things of national importance will crowd on the attention of Parliament for the East of London to get even a passing notice.' Booth could not but take notice. 'The people are starving in Poplar,' he commented. 'Visiting is almost impossible without the means of relieving the people . . . I had thought of giving up the soup kitchen, but am assured that the soup and the bread given with it are all that many poor creatures have to eat the day through.'

As often happens, it only needed some good to be done for it to be ill spoken of. Early in 1868 *The Saturday Review* charged the Mission with misusing monies subscribed to 'tempt the poor to worship by the bait of a breakfast and coal ticket.' All that Booth could do was to repeat that never had attendance at any meeting, nor any profession of faith, been required as a prior condition of receiving help — and to press on undeterred with plans to develop the relief work centred on the People's Market which had been acquired and re-opened on April 10th, 1870, as the People's Mission Hall. Existing facilities at the hall were supplemented by the opening of food shops — at one time there were five of these — for the provision of cheap meals. James Flawn, one of the original tent workers, reported that —

> during the short time this has been opened we have supplied 5,000 families with soup and bread free . . . We sell soup to between six hundred and a thousand persons daily at one penny per pint, and a large slice of bread for one half-penny — much of which is taken home to families . . . We sell a pint of tea for three half-pence . . . coffee for one penny per pint . . . large quantities of boiled and baked pudding at a penny a large slice.

The one mistake — if it can be so called — was that William Booth's reach was exceeding his grasp — though who can blame him for that? Overwork took its inevitable toll and, not for the first time, complete rest was the only cure. His eldest son, Bramwell, still a teenager, was called upon to oversee this relief work as best he could. Thanks be to God, Flawn continued as his principal helper, and few managers were as dedicated as he. The feeding operations were intended to be self-supporting, but losses began to mount and by the middle of 1877 William Booth had to advise the Whitechapel secretary of the Charity Organisation Society that he could no longer undertake general relief work.

Something must now be said about this society, for William Booth and his works frequently came under its condemnation. In 1869 the name of the existing 'Association for the prevention of pauperism and crime' was changed to the 'Society for organising charitable relief and repressing mendicity' — in short, the Charity Organisation Society, widely known by its initials. In the society's view one of the principal causes of pauperism was ill-judged and ill-regulated charity, and consequently its main object was

to provide 'machinery for systematising, without unduly
controlling, the benevolence of the public.' With this in
mind local committees were set up and honorary sec-
retaries installed so that the society might succeed in its self-
appointed task of unifying charitable policy and practice.
Indiscriminate charity only increased the sum total of
poverty and must therefore be condemned as doing overall
more harm than good.

Certain of the doctrines of the C.O.S. could not be
faulted — provided that the social structure of the day was
accepted as the best in the best of all possible worlds. With
'the rich man in his castle' and 'the poor man at his gate',
charity was held to be a blessed bond between giver and
receiver. Improvidence was not to be countenanced, and
certainly not to be encouraged, by casual giving. Any overlapping by one charitable society of the work of another
was an open invitation to the scrounger to exploit to his
advantage.

All this was true — as far as it went, but the C.O.S. could
not — or would not — see that industrial poverty in an
urban society was not necessarily due to individual failure,
or that personal inadequacy was the major cause of social
destitution. William Booth was not a professional economist, but it was plain to him that —

> most schemes that are put forward for the improvement
> of the people . . . would only affect the aristocracy of the
> miserable. It is the thrifty, the industrious, the sober, the
> thoughtful who can take advantage of these plans . . . No
> one will ever make a visible dent on the mass of squalor
> who does not deal with the improvident, the lazy, the
> vicious, the criminal. The scheme of social salvation is not
> worth discussing which is not as wide as the scheme of
> eternal salvation.

In other words, the 'undeserving' poor were not to be
passed by on the other side. 'To attempt to save the lost,'

countered Booth, 'we must accept no limitations of human brotherhood.'

This was heresy to the C.O.S. Such 'open-handed, undiscriminating charity cut at the root of all their teaching and endeavours.' And C. S. Loch, a Balliol man who succeeded Charles Bosanquet as the society's paid secretary in 1875, though possessing gifts of the highest order, was equally rigid in his outlook. Even soup kitchens came under his ban, for no attempt was made to distinguish between 'deserving' and 'undeserving' applicants. When, by bringing together in the same schools children of varying social backgrounds, the 1870 Education Act revealed the link between physical health and the capacity to learn, Loch would not hear of the provision of free or cheap meals. All such projects should be self-supporting. The needs of the children who were destitute should be met by the Poor Law. Those whose parents were ill should be given family relief. To feed children whose parents were neglectful or thriftless was to invite such people to spend in idleness or drink the money which should have been devoted to the upkeep of their family. As many of the active members of the C.O.S. were drawn from the professions, the armed forces and the civil service, led by a highly articulate secretary, Booth faced formidable criticism. He rarely wasted time in self-justification, though he was stung into saying that 'the Charity Organisation Society believes in the survival of the fit . . . We believe in the survival of the unfit.'

It might seem to a superficial observer that over this period William Booth was losing interest in social welfare, but it should be remembered that he was grappling with the orderly organisation of a Movement which, unless adequately structured, could outgrow its strength. By the end of 1883 — five years after the change of name from The Christian Mission to The Salvation Army, the fifty stations (or corps) of June, 1878, had become more than five hundred, and by 1886 had risen to over a thousand. Within the same period of time, the work of the Army had spread to

North America, Australia, imperial India, South Africa and western Europe. The opportunities for social service varied from country to country, but such as were presented were grasped. For instance, new ground was broken in Melbourne (Victoria) by the opening on December 8th, 1883, of a reception centre for discharged prisoners. Within four years five such centres had been set up in the state capital, and Booth dispatched an officer from England to Australia to study how this development could be applied to the home base.

Almost simultaneously the experiment of appointing women officers to live and work in the heart of slum areas was begun in Walworth. By 1887 six other downtown centres had been opened in the capital, and in another two years similar work was commenced in Glasgow, Liverpool, Manchester and Nottingham.

Nor should it be forgotten that this decade was one of severe persecution for Salvationists in many parts of the United Kingdom. Certain provincial magistrates announced their refusal to give these 'disturbers of the peace' the due protection of the law, and refused to convict those guilty of assaulting them — until the Lord Chief Justice reminded the courts of their public duty.

Booth could have had enough troubles on his own plate not to bother with other people's, but human need was never far from his thoughts. During this brief interregnum he was but girding himself to grapple in an even more thorough-going manner with the inarticulate misery of the poor, even though sentence of death had just been passed upon his beloved Catherine. He was to lose her on October 4th, 1890.

Nevertheless at the beginning of 1888 *The War Cry* announced the opening of a 'sleeping shelter' in the West India Dock Road where soup would be supplied to children at a farthing a basin; soup and bread for a halfpenny. Booth was not the originator of such relief. A chain of soup kitchens had been opened in London in 1796 to meet the exceptional distress of the time. But when the need recurred Flawn came into his own again, and before the first week was out hundreds of adults and children were being fed daily — with the result that two further centres of the same kind were opened in St. John's Square and Lisson Street respectively.

Victorian complacency was not greatly ruffled. The Home Secretary told the Queen that the London poor were no worse off than they had been. It was the foreign visitor who was appalled by what many a resident took for granted. Exiled in London during the middle of the century, Gavarni could write with horrified amazement: '*Il est vraiment possible de mourir de faim*'. (It is actually possible to die of hunger.) Official figures reported forty-eight deaths from starvation in London in 1898; thirty-nine in 1903; forty-two even in 1910.

Behind every statistic was a story as, for example, that of James Theade, aged sixty-two, journeyman bootmaker, who was found lying in the New Cut on December 28th, 1898, at 1:50 a.m. He told a constable that he had sought admission to the local casual ward, but because he had fourpence in his pocket he was not allowed in. He then tried for shelter in a common lodging house, but it was full. He died in the Lambeth Infirmary at 6 a.m. the same morning. The cause of death was given as acute congestion of the lungs, due to exposure and want.

At the inquest on James Greaves, carman, living at Vine Court, Whitechapel, his widow stated that he had been out of work for some time and they had little food in the house. The deceased became so ill that she obtained a parish order and took him to the infirmary. The Medical Officer deposed that death was due to influenza and pneumonia, aggravated by want of food.

A widow, Eliza Topping, died three-quarters of an hour after admission to the infirmary. The coroner's officer testified that she and her two sons lived in a top floor back room measuring twelve feet by eight, containing one broken chair, two old cans, and one 2' 9" bed in which all three slept. Her body was in an advanced state of emaciation. There was no fat anywhere on what was virtually a skeleton, and the deceased could not have eaten for the previous four days*.

Nor were these isolated instances. The unemployment figures which' had fallen between 1894 and 1899 began to rise again nationwide between 1900 and 1904, in addition to which the winter of 1905/6 was one of exceptional severity. Schemes of relief were proposed with fervour and opposed with equal vehemence. There was talk of a session of Parliament being summoned to consider the creation of public work schemes. But in those more leisurely days the Leader of the Opposition feared that it would be difficult to collect a sufficient number of M.P.'s to hold a session, and the Prime Minister opined that while parliamentary proceedings were 'invaluable for the purpose of criticising legislative proposals or executive action, and might prepare the way for a constructive policy, they could hardly frame one.' It was left to *The Social Gazette* to comment, with justifiable acerbity, that 'there seemed little else for the unemployed to do but to get through the winter as best they could with the aid of soup kitchens and cheap meals.'

This is more or less what happened. The scandal of the starving was not confined to London, but in the capital it was impossible for the press to ignore the way in which Booth and his officers were doing their utmost to stab the national conscience broad awake. Not that they were always thanked for their self-imposed labour of love, but there were moments when even the ranks of Tuscany were compelled to cheer — witness the following condensed extract from *The Times* quoted by *The Social Gazette* of November 26th, 1904.

The present distress in London may or may not be more acute than in 1895 but there is, unfortunately, not the slightest doubt that it is widespread. In these circumstances it can hardly be wrong if I give an account of a

* *The Social Gazette*, March 16th, 1895; October 2nd, 1897 and October 28th, 1899.

night spent with The Salvation Army, watching in detail the operation which they have undertaken to meet some of the most pressing cases in this accumulation of misery.

It is also fair to The Salvation Army to say, by way of preface, that I am constitutionally averse to 'corybantic Christianity', that I detest many of their methods, and that I am convinced of the unsoundness of many of their social principles.

At a quarter to one yesterday morning I made my way to their establishment in Stanhope Street, Drury Lane, and thence into the highways with sheaves of soup tickets which were offered to all sorts and conditions of men. It was about as filthy and raw a night as the heart of a hater of humanity could desire.

Down the Strand we passed, up into Trafalgar Square, through Leicester Square and through some of the choicest parts of Seven Dials back to Stanhope Street. There, waiting in queue, like those who desire to enter the pit of a popular theatre, were some hundreds of men and women who were unquestionably destitute and homeless. They were of all ages, plenty of them were able bodied, few of them were very badly dressed, though practically none was adequately protected against the weather.

To each in turn was given a bowl of soup and a hunk of bread; each then took a spoon from a basket lying on the pavement, and a pinch of salt from a bowl, and then moved into a side street to consume the meal. The women were allowed to sit and eat inside the building. The order maintained was perfect, and each man, when he had finished, returned his bowl and spoon and passed into the damp darkness of the night. It was, without any affectation, a spectacle upon which it was impossible for an Englishman to look without deep sorrow. It was appalling to see these men filing away into the slush and darkness.

So to Whitechapel, where the story was the same, save that the individuals were other men and women — ship's stewards, stokers, grocer's employees, labourers, masons, photographic artists, doctors of medicine, labourers of all kinds. Here we tasted some of the soup, which was excellent stuff, 'with some heart in it.'

Firm believer as I am in political economy, abundantly convinced that the work done cannot go far in the direction of redeeming the fortunes of the men and women who are submerged, I cannot deny that the work which is being done is distinctly good. For all that the duty to feed the hungry is imperative, and there is no doubt that The Salvation Army offers a channel through which this can be fulfilled.

Even the City of London gave two cheers — by making a grant of £100 so that this food distribution work might continue. Perhaps the city fathers remembered that hungry men are often angry men, and in the month of January alone 32,000 of them were fed at Stanhope Street and Whitechapel. Keir Hardie thought that this was a task for the central government — as indeed it was. But he added: 'This is Christlike work, and I trust that ample funds will be provided to enable the Army to continue it. He must have a heart of stone who, having the means, withholds his help from such a labour of love as this.'

And continued it was — both in London and the main provincial cities up to the First World War, when the shape of human need, as well as the means of meeting it, suffered a change. Until then the following word picture written in the winter of 1907 by a *Daily Mail* reporter held good.

Nearly every face was thin, and every pair of eyes sunken. Boys were there who had come up to make their fortunes in London; some old men as well, but most were in the prime of years. Many of the faces looked extremely intelligent. All were tired out for all had been walking the streets the entire day. Some nodded even before they had finished their substantial basin of soup. Some greedily devoured the food and then sank to the floor in exhaustion ...

It was awesome to note how silent they were. There were no jokes and there was no roughness. The only laugh was when the Captain tried to show his humour in order to raise their spirits. The men may have thought it was their duty to laugh. A stranger might have thought that their laughter was a half sob.

A ball by ball commentary covering these years would be wearisome. One free meal is very much like the next. But in contrast to Jack London's strictures on Salvation Army service, a London author, Dennis Crane, visited a metropolitan shelter incognito, and wrote:

> For twopence a man can buy a nourishing meal. I had a mug of tea and a thick slice of bread and butter for a penny. This I supplemented with a large plateful of mashed potatoes as white as flour and haricot beans. Over the whole was poured a ladleful of thick gravy. This cost one penny. Nowhere in London could the value be surpassed, or even equalled.

But more than adults were starving. Small children could not escape what their parents had to endure. Official statistics estimated that even in 1908 3,000 children in London went to school without breakfast. The figure for England and Wales was 120,000. The Provision of Meals Act (effective January 1st, 1908) empowered local authorities to provide out of rate money for the feeding of children who, through poverty, were compelled to attend school 'in a state of hunger.' The loophole was that the Act only allowed — not required — local authorities to do so, and the majority of them took no action whatever. Before the turn of the century the Army had been providing farthing breakfasts in most towns of any size and, with the passing of this Act planned to discontinue this service. When the local authorities fell down on the job the breakfasts were resumed. Just under half-a-million were served in the first winter in London alone.

It was about this time that a school inspector was questioning in class a boy who came from a Salvationist home. Exceeding his brief somewhat the visitor said: 'Your people do not have the Lord's Supper.'

'No, sir.'

'Then what do they put in its place?'

'Farthing breakfasts for starving children, sir.'

Out of the mouth of babes and sucklings!

4

Truth Fallen in the Street

William Booth shared in one other major social reform before the publication of *In Darkest England and the Way Out* in October, 1890. This was the raising of the age of consent.

While England was still involved in the Napoleonic wars the Guardian Society was investigating how best to rid the streets of prostitutes and to provide homes for those who wished to change their way of life. In the opening in Glasgow in May, 1883, of the Army's first rescue home for women Booth shared the concern of many nineteenth-century church folk. High Church sisterhoods set up reception centres, though one group thus employed bore the forbidding title of the Church Penitentiary Association. Some evangelicals took to the highways and byways of the larger cities in order to gather in such 'fallen women' — the most frequently used Victorian euphemism — who wished to abandon the streets. Catherine Booth, William's wife, shared in this Midnight Movement (as it was called), and along with such well-known church figures as Newman Hall and Baptist Noel addressed late night gatherings.

Commented *The Methodist Times*: 'The address of Mrs. Booth was inimitable ... She identified herself with her hearers as a fellow sinner, showing that if they supposed her better than themselves it was a mistake, since all had sinned against God. This (she explained) was the main point, and not the particular sin of which they might have been guilty.'

Any official initiative in this field by William Booth had been anticipated in 1881 by a largely forgotten woman

Salvationist, Mrs. Cottrill, living at 102 Christian Street,
Whitechapel. She was the 'Converts' Sergeant' at the Whitechapel corps — that is, hers was the responsibility to care
for those who made a profession of faith in Jesus as Saviour
and Lord at the local meetings. The cause of immediate
urgency was a country girl who had come up to London in
search of domestic service but who, lured by a false address,
found herself in a brothel. After kneeling at the Mercy Seat
she could not return to a disorderly house. Where then could
she stay? Mrs. Cottrill had a simple answer. She took her
home.

If one girl had been thus trapped there were without doubt
many others in a similar plight, and this unsophisticated
mother of five children saw that their first need was a refuge
where they would be received with uncritical compassion.
Her house had a basement which she cleared and made
ready for any such unexpected but never unwelcome
visitors and, when this work of love and mercy became more
than she could sustain single-handedly, turned for advice
to William Booth's eldest son, Bramwell, who asked her to
try to find some other premises which could be rented by
the Army for this purpose. After no small searching Mrs.
Cottrill found an empty house in Hanbury Street at a rent
of twenty-five shillings a week. Mrs. William Booth picked
up some secondhand furniture in a sale room. Spare chairs
were secured from a nearby Army hall. Bedding was
improvised. Some of the girls for whom Mrs. Cottrill was
already caring helped to prepare the house for occupation,
and William Booth placed his daughter-in-law, Mrs. Bramwell Booth, in charge of this shoestring enterprise which was
full to overflowing with thirteen or fourteen occupants by
day and eight by night.

Mrs. Cottrill did not cease from her beneficent labour for
now she patrolled the Ratcliff Highway — 'that reservoir
of dirt, drunkenness and drabs' as Dickens called it —
which ran from the Royal Mint to Limehouse, announcing
the existence of this shelter for needy women and girls.

She had a plenteous constituency for, of the seven hundred odd dwellings in four of the streets adjacent to St. George's-in-the-East, more than a hundred and fifty were brothels. Not surprisingly, the necessity for such primitive publicity soon ceased, for within four months word was issued that no more girls were to be sent to Hanbury Street without prior assurance that there was room for them. It was from this admittedly unprepossessing refuge that Bramwell Booth, through his young wife, began to grasp the extent of child prostitution and 'resolved ... no matter what the consequences ... to do all I could ... to rouse public opinion, to agitate for the improvement of the law, to bring to justice the murderers of innocence, and to make a way of escape for the victims.'

Prostitutes in general followed their calling more openly in Victorian times than at almost any other period in English history. So far as child prostitution was concerned the report of a Select Committee of the House of Lords had already declared that —

the evidence before the Committee proves beyond all doubt that juvenile prostitution, from an almost incredibly early age, is increasing to an appalling extent in England, and especially in London. The Committee is unable adequately to express its sense of the magnitude, both from a moral and a physical point of view, of the evil thus brought to light, and of the necessity for taking vigorous measures to cope with it.

One of the Committee's principal recommendations was that 'the age up to which it shall be an offence to have or attempt to have carnal knowledge of, or to indecently assault a girl, be raised from thirteen to sixteen.'

It is currently supposed in some quarters that the age of consent has been — and should be — related to the age of puberty. This has not been the position in the United Kingdom in the past. The Offences against the Person Act of

1861 made twelve the age of consent, for that was the age
at which, by common law, a girl could marry. But that is
not to say that every girl of twelve years of age was mature
enough for marriage. In 1871 a Royal Commission proposed
that the age of consent be raised to fourteen, but in 1875
this was fixed at thirteen. However, in 1883 a Bill embodying
the recommendation of the Lords' Committee was passed
by the Upper House but came to grief in the Commons.
The following year the Bill was reintroduced in the Lords,
passed and sent down to the Commons, but this time it
perished in the conflict between the two Houses over the
County Franchise Bill which the Liberal Government of
that day had promoted. Yet a third time the Bill to raise the
age of consent was presented to the Lords, and the second
reading in the Commons was moved by the Home Secretary
himself. But barely a quorum of members were present and
they were divided among themselves. One honourable
member made the point that there were girls of twelve who
were very precocious, in which situation it was the man
himself who might need protection! The debate was
adjourned, and the House rose without setting any date for
a resumption of discussion on the measure. The Bill was as
good as dead.

But three figures had joined forces. One was the brave
and beautiful Josephine Butler, wife of the Anglican George
Butler, later Canon of Winchester. Said one eye-witness of
her in her late fifties: 'Her face was framed on pure and
beautiful lines, but . . . it had seen that which took all the
colour and joy out of it.' Like a first century believer, Mrs.
Butler bore the marks of the Lord Jesus, the outward and
visible signs of all she had inwardly endured in defence of
the defenceless. Hers had been a lonely battle with few allies
— either male or female. Even as level-headed a women's
leader as Millicent Fawcett had refused to share in her
crusade against licensed prostitution lest such action prejudice the crusade for the vote. Nevertheless Mrs. Butler
continued her campaign for the repeal of the Contagious

Diseases Act, addressing street meetings and tendering evidence before government committees with equal resolution and skill. It was while waiting to appear before one such committee that she wrote to her husband: 'I will tell you when we meet of my going to one of The Salvation Army meetings to refresh my soul. It was lovely. No peeresses there, but the humblest people with faces radiant with happiness.'

The second was a Congregational minister's son, William T. Stead, who after serving as editor of *The Northern Echo* in Darlington, came to London in 1880 as associate editor to John Morley on the *Pall Mall Gazette*, succeeding him three years later. Virtually alone among the national newspapers Stead took the Commons to task for failing to pass the Criminal Law Amendment Act. Most of the London press looked firmly the other way. It was unthinkable that the Victorian taboo upon any public discussion of the ethics of sex should be broken. Smut might freely be retailed in club smoking rooms; the Burlington Arcade be described as 'the western counterpart of an eastern slave market'; but any serious discussion — especially by women — of the cause and cure of promiscuity was positively indecent.

Such false delicacy could not be laid to the charge of The Salvation Army which, in the person of Bramwell Booth, supplied the third member of the trio. At first he had been inclined to discount as exaggerated the stories which his wife told him. Some young girls were notoriously fanciful. But the last of his hesitations disappeared when an attractive girl of seventeen was found waiting in the early morning at the door of the Army's headquarters in London. Hers was an all too familiar tale. She had come up to the capital in response to an advertisement, found herself in a brothel and, in her dilemma, recalled that in her box was a cheap Salvation Army song book which bore the name and address of General William Booth. He would surely help her. At four o'clock in the morning she stole out of the house and walked from Pimlico to 101 Queen Victoria Street. Enquiries confirmed the truth of her story and this, together with the testimony of a number of young girls whom his wife brought up from Hanbury Street determined him to consult Josephine Butler and one of her principal helpers, Benjamin Scott, the Quaker Chamberlain of the City of London, and then to acquaint W. T. Stead with 'the facts of child enslavement and prostitution as they had come to his notice.'

The Butlers had been out-and-out supporters of the anti-slavery cause in the U.S.A., and knew how the Abolitionists had themselves purchased negro slaves in order to set them free. Was not a parallel course of action possible in Britain? But how? Bramwell Booth was to supply the answer for to Hanbury Street had come Rebecca Jarrett, thirty-six years of age, sick in body and mind for she herself, seduced when the age of consent was still twelve, had kept brothels in London, Bristol and Manchester, and was now reaping the tragic harvest of her way of life.

One evening she crept unobserved into a Salvation Army meeting in Northampton but, overcome by the heat of the crowded room, fainted. This brought to her side the woman officer who was leading the meeting. Rebecca could not escape her gentle importunity, if only because her current male companion was more than willing to offload a woman whose personal charms were plainly fading. The woman Captain brought her to Hanbury Street where Mrs. Bramwell Booth arranged for her to have essential medical treatment at the London Hospital, and then saw that Rebecca's chances of making good would be greatly aided if she left London. In the city her old friends were too handy; her old way of life was too readily available. Mrs. William Booth interceded with Mrs. Butler who agreed to take the repentant Rebecca into her own refuge in Winchester, where in due season she began to work out her own salvation by helping young teenage girls who themselves were in moral danger. Would not a woman who knew the trade from the inside be the very one to help Stead to expose it?

Only with the greatest reluctance did Rebecca yield to

Stead's insistence that she should help him demonstrate to the British public how easy it was to buy a girl of thirteen for immoral purposes. From long experience Rebecca knew the hazards of such an undertaking as Stead did not. Well for him to secure his position by advising the Archbishop of Canterbury in advance of his intentions, gain the support of Frederick Temple, recently appointed Bishop of London, receive the unqualified blessing of Cardinal Manning, not to mention the full assurances of both Mrs. Butler and the Booths that Rebecca — despite her manifest unwillingness — would not let him down.

Rebecca had no such powerful defenders, and felt in her bones that she would not be able to re-enter the unsavoury world she had so recently left and emerge unscathed. She had lived in it too long not to know the gins and snares hidden in the seemingly innocuous language of human barter. In her own inarticulate way she had no wish even to consider using Satan's methods to cast out Satan. But she could not withstand Stead — few people could — so finally she found a poor girl, Eliza Armstrong, thirteen years of age, and supposed — as money had changed hands — that her parents had consented to part with their daughter. But all her dealings had been with Eliza's mother, and only indirectly with the father through the mother; never at first hand. This was the joint in her armour — and in Stead's as well. A child was abducted from her home without her father's consent. In the eyes of the law this was an offence. But of this fatal flaw in his carefully planned scheme Stead had no premonition when the first of his ten articles under the general title of 'The Maiden Tribute of Modern Babylon' appeared in the *Pall Mall Gazette* for Monday, July 6th, 1885.

The run on the paper beggared description for Stead did not limit himself to what he had learned from The Salvation Army. He gave the trade the full treatment, with the result that it needed a posse of police to keep clear the entrance to the offices of the *Gazette* in Northumberland Avenue. When

W. H. Smith banned the paper from his bookstalls because of its alleged indecency, William Booth opened his headquarters as a distribution centre. When demand exceeded supply, newsboys reaped their own harvest by charging half-a-crown a copy. When manpower ran short, G. B. Shaw offered to hawk around the streets as many copies as he could carry.

Nor were Stead's supporters slow to rally to his side. To those who questioned the wisdom of his disclosures, William Booth said bluntly that they seemed to him more like complaints about the dogs who were barking than the wolves who were biting. 'I think the time has come,' he said to a politically minded friend, 'that you politicians should have another party — one based on morality ... Whatever differences of opinion there may be with regard to forms of government, there can be no difference of opinion that a good government ought to be the father of its people and the protector of their children.'

Mass meetings were held in London and the provinces, and in one such in the Prince's Hall, Piccadilly, Mrs. William Booth flayed those Members of Parliament who had argued that some young girls were too forward and contended that the age of consent should be reduced to ten.

I read some paragraphs from the report of a debate in the House of Commons which made me doubt my eyesight ... I did not think we were so low as this — that one member should suggest that the age of these innocents ... should be reduced to ten and, O my God!, pleaded that it was hard for a man — hard, for a man — having a charge brought against him, not to be able to plead the consent of a child like that.

Well may the higher classes take care of their little girls! Well may they be so careful never to let them go out without efficient protectors: But what is to become of the little girls of the poor? Of the little girls of the working classes? I could not have believed that in this country such a discussion among so-called gentlemen could have taken place.

Twice Mrs. Booth wrote to Queen Victoria and once to Prime Minister Gladstone. Her first letter read:

May it please Your Majesty:

My heart has been so filled with distress and apprehension on account of the rejection by the House of Commons of the Bill for the Protection of Young Girls from the consequences of male profligacy that, on behalf of tens of thousands of the most pitiable and helpless of Your Majesty's subjects, I venture to address you.

First, I would pray that Your Majesty will cause the Bill to be re-introduced during the present session of Parliament, and —

Secondly, I would pray Your Majesty to be graciously pleased to insist on the age limit being fixed at sixteen . . .

If only I could convey to Your Majesty an idea of the tenth part of the demoralisation, shame and suffering entailed on thousands of the children of the poor by the present state of the law on this subject, I feel sure that your womanly feelings would be roused to indignation, and Your Majesty would make the remaining years of your glorious reign (which I fervently pray may be many) even more illustrious than those that are past . . . in order to save the female children of your people . . .

Through the Dowager Duchess Roxburgh the Queen assured Mrs. Booth that she 'fully sympathised (with her) on the painful subject to which she referred, and had already communicated thereon with a lady closely connected with the Government, to whom Mrs. Booth's letter would at once be forwarded.'

The current parliamentary session was far spent but Mrs. Booth begged Gladstone to reintroduce the Criminal Law Amendment Bill. 'I think I may truthfully say,' she wrote, 'that I represent hundreds of thousands of the working class in this request for I have ample evidence that, if they were appealed to, their voices would be raised as one man in seconding this request.'

By this time there was no holding her. 'Powerful with her pen,' wrote her son-in-law biographer, Booth-Tucker, 'she was well nigh irresistible on the platform' — and the prospect of further public rallies throughout the country stirred her so deeply that once more she wrote to the Queen begging that Her Majesty —

> would at this juncture graciously send us a word of sympathy and encouragement to be read at our mass meetings to be held in different parts of the kingdom, the first of which takes place on Thursday evening next at the Exeter Hall.
>
> Allow me to add that it would cheer Your Majesty's heart to hear the response of immense audiences in different parts of the land when it is intimated that the heart of Your Majesty beats in sympathy with this effort to protect and rescue the juvenile daughters of your people . . .

To this the Dowager Marchioness of Ely replied that she 'need scarcely tell Mrs. Booth that the Queen feels very deeply on the subject to which her letter refers, but Her Majesty has been advised that it would not be desirable for the Queen to express an opinion on a matter which forms at present the object of a measure before Parliament.'

Fair enough; the Bill had not yet been talked out. But there were other ways of rousing public opinion and, within seventeen days of the proposal being mooted, a petition bearing 393,000 signatures was conveyed through London to Trafalgar Square, accompanied by an escort of mothers and the men cadets' band. To comply with the law that no procession should approach within a mile of Westminster when the House was in session, the petition was then carried down Whitehall on the shoulders of eight cadets and, laid on the floor of the House because there was not sufficient room on the customary Commons table, prayed that:

1. The age of responsibility for young girls should be raised to eighteen.
2. Procuration of young people for ... immoral purposes should be made a criminal offence.
3. Power should be given to a magistrate to order entry into any house where there was reason to believe that any girl under age was being detained there against her will, and —
4. Men and women should be equal before the law; that is, as it is a criminal offence for a woman to solicit a man, it shall be equally criminal for a man to solicit a woman.

The same day as Stead's first article appeared in the *Pall Mall Gazette*, the new Prime Minister, Lord Salisbury, faced the Commons. Three days later the Home Secretary rose to say that it had been decided to resume the debate on the Criminal Law Amendment Bill, for which the Government would give the fullest facilities. The Bill was given a third reading by 179 votes to 71, and on August 14th received the Royal Assent.

A backlash was inevitable. Eliza Armstrong's mother had neighbours who also read the *Pall Mall Gazette*. Though Stead had called Eliza 'Lily', they soon suspected the truth. Some newspapers wrote off Stead's story as fiction. This neighbourhood was sure it was fact, and before long Mrs. Armstrong was seeking the assistance of the Marylebone police court to recover her lost child. One day a reporter from *Lloyds' Newspaper* — a Sunday rival of the *Gazette* — happened to be around, and to him Mrs. Armstrong unburdened her heart. He also knew a good story when he heard one. A loving mother was looking for her missing daughter. Where was Eliza?

Eliza had not been harmed — despite a succession of experiences which could have bewildered — even frightened

— her. She had been bought a new outfit in which — to add an undesirable but unhappily essential verisimilitude to the whole exercise — she had been taken to an establishment in Milton Street where she was examined by a midwife. From thence she was brought by arrangement to a house of assignation which Stead himself briefly visited. In the care of a trusted woman Salvation Army officer, Major Mrs. Reynolds, the girl made yet one more call — this time to a specialist who certified that she was *virgo intacta*. These were steps parallel to those taken by any procuress of that day to meet the needs of her clients.

So far, so good? But at this juncture Stead changed his mind and, instead of sending Eliza in Rebecca's care to the Butlers' refuge in Winchester, decided that the girl should leave the country in order to be out of her mother's reach. Again Bramwell Booth came to his aid and asked Madame Combe, a Swiss widow of independent means who was in the Army's service in Clapton, to take the girl over to France. But by now Eliza did not want to leave Rebecca, and so all three left together for Paris, though later Rebecca returned to Winchester and Eliza went farther south to relatives of Madame Combe in Loriol.

But *Lloyds'* were on the trail, and this early instance of what is now styled 'investigative reporting' was beginning to pay off. Public interest was maintained throughout July by the appearance of articles which were based on little more than half a fact and a couple of rumours. The *St. James Gazette* — another paper antagonistic to The Salvation Army — entered the fray with dark hints of hidden links between Rebecca Jarrett, the Butlers at Winchester, and the Army. But *Lloyds'* was not going to allow any other dog to walk off with their bone. With a great show of righteousness the paper demanded that Mrs. Armstrong should see General Booth himself and insist on her daughter's return. So when Eliza's mother next went to Marylebone, the magistrates sent her to Queen Victoria Street — and an inspector with her. They were given Eliza's address, but nearly another three weeks passed — with *Lloyds'* keeping the fires of public curiosity well and truly stoked — before the Home Office awoke to the fact that Charles Armstrong was the presumed father of the missing child and sent him, accompanied by another police inspector, to Loriol. In the interim — for all the parties in this Box and Cox affair were working independently of one another — Eliza had returned to London and was happily lodged with the Steads at Wimbledon whence, on the appearance of her mother, she returned home safe and well with her wages paid in full. A detailed account of this happy ending appeared in *Lloyds'*. The paper's disinterested objective had been secured. Mother and child were reunited.

Happy ending? Hardly for all who were involved for Mr. Cavendish Bentinck, another determined critic of the Army, had already risen in the House to ask whether the Home Secretary's attention had been drawn to the information which had appeared in *Lloyds' Newspaper* and, if so, what action did he propose to take? Another member asked whether a felony had not been committed, for which those responsible should be prosecuted. The Home Secretary replied that he had already sought the opinion of the Attorney General and, on September 8th, W. T. Stead, Rebecca Jarrett, Bramwell Booth, Madame Combe, Jacques (one of Stead's assistants) and Madame Mourez (the midwife) were charged at Bow Street under Section 56, 24 & 25 Vict., C. 100, an Act of 1861 entitled Offences against the Person, with the abduction of Eliza Armstrong from the care of her father. When proceedings began, however, the Attorney General announced that he had now decided to proceed under section 55 which made it a misdemeanour to abduct an unmarried girl under sixteen. To this was added the charge of 'aiding and abetting an indecent assault on Eliza Armstrong.'

Public opinion was fiercely divided. On the first day of the hearing the defendants were hissed in court. A mob paraded outside the Bow Street station carrying effigies of Stead. The police told Bramwell Booth that, for his own safety, he should take off his uniform when leaving the court. Even a cab gave no protection, and a Black Maria provided by the police proved a welcome shelter. Salvation Army meetings were frequently interrupted with the cry: 'What about Eliza Armstrong?' By contrast, on the evening before the Old Bailey hearings began, William Booth led a half-night of prayer in the Clapton Congress Hall which was shared by Salvation Army congregations all over the world. The burden of this united act of intercession was not that any of the accused might be delivered from imprisonment, but that in each of their lives the will of the Lord should be done.

This was a genuine act of faith for, while some of the provincial papers were sympathetic, the major part of the London press was hostile to Stead. In their eyes he deserved his come-uppance. Professional jealousy was undoubtedly a factor here. Both judges also made very plain what they thought of the *Pall Mall* articles, though their contents were not at all relevant to the charges before the court. Nevertheless the Bow Street magistrate described them as 'deplorable and nauseous'; the Old Bailey judge as 'disgusting and filthy'. Neither would allow any evidence with regard to motive. The Archbishop of Canterbury was present at the Old Bailey ready to testify on Stead's behalf, but though His Grace was given a seat on the bench he was not allowed into the witness box. Motive could not be taken into account. The law was not to be broken even by good men with the best of intentions. 'I shall tell the jury,' said Mr. Justice Lopes, 'that whosoever takes away a child from its father does so at his peril.' By that ruling the case was finally lost, though not a word was allowed to be said about the extent of child prostitution which was the over-riding cause of this technical abduction.

All the same, the public at large continued to insist on being heard. On Thursday, October 15th, in the gap between the two trials, the Exeter Hall in London was filled for the final rally arranged by the National Vigilance Association in support of Stead. Among those on the platform were Hugh Price Hughes and Josephine Butler, and the Methodist leader announced that this was the last of the public demonstrations which had been held over the previous twelve days in Darlington, South Shields, Newcastle, Leeds, Bradford, Sheffield, Manchester and Leicester. A message of support was read from Charles Spurgeon, and reference was made to a declaration signed by nearly four hundred Anglican clergy, more than eight hundred Methodist and just under six hundred Baptist ministers, together with another five hundred church leaders of other denominations, deploring the use of public funds and time to prosecute those who had exposed a national scandal and ensured a public remedy.

Mrs. William Booth once again assailed the Home Secretary — this time on behalf of Rebecca Jarrett, who (she wrote) —

was herself a victim of male criminality at the age of fifteen, and lived an immoral life for fourteen years, the greater part of which time she kept a brothel and was allowed to prosecute her vile trade without the interference of the law. Nine months ago this woman was rescued by The Salvation Army, and has since lived an entirely changed life . . .

She is now in solitary confinement in a stone cell, with only a mat to lie on, without bed or pillow, her own warm clothing having been taken away, leaving her shivering with cold by day and night, notwithstanding that she is suffering from incurable hip disease, having left the hospital only a few months.

Jarrett gave herself up voluntarily twenty-four hours after she knew that a warrant had been issued for her arrest; nevertheless she was not allowed bail, although a brothel keeper charged with keeping a disorderly house was granted that privilege the day before . . .

I cannot believe, Sir Richard, that you will allow such an injustice to continue . . . and praying that you will give immediate orders for the amelioration of Jarrett's surroundings,

I am, Sir . . .

Even as the Old Bailey proceedings were drawing to a close Mrs. Booth telegraphed the Queen at length. Agree with it or not, this deserves to be quoted in full for its direct and fearless language.

May it please Your Majesty to allow me to state that I know W. T. Stead, whose prosecution has been instigated by the hate and revenge of bad men, to be one of the bravest and most righteous men in Your Majesty's dominions, and if tomorrow he should be sentenced to imprisonment it will shock and arouse millions of your best and most loyal subjects to the highest indignation.

I pray by all the love I bear Your Majesty, and by all the pity I feel for your outraged infant subjects, that you will, if possible, interfere to avert such a calamity. May God endue Your Majesty with wisdom and strength to ignore all evil counsellors, and to exert your royal prerogative for the deliverance of those who are persecuted only for righteousness' sake, prays your loyal and devoted servant in Jesus,

Catherine Booth.

But as Lady Longford makes clear in her *Victoria, R.I.* —

Stead and the *Pall Mall* were more than Her Majesty could stomach. She drafted a harsh telegram to Mrs. Booth (afterwards softened by Ponsonby), pointing out that Stead's case was still *sub judice*, and she could not interfere.

This tempered reply read:

The Queen has received your telegram. It is well understood that Her Majesty cannot interfere in the proceedings of any trial while it is still going on. If necessary, an appeal through the Secretary of State can be made to the Queen for a remission of sentence.

Nothing daunted, Mrs. Booth wrote once more to Sir Richard Cross, the Home Secretary, pleading that though Stead and Jarrett 'may have been guilty of a technical breach of the law, they were actuated by the highest motives.' In his official biography of Mrs. Booth, Frederick Booth-Tucker takes the view that the Queen 'would have gladly granted the countless petitions which poured in upon her . . . but precedent and the constitution left her powerless to follow out her own convictions.' This is a moot point.

It is true (Lady Longford has written) that the Queen's feelings about prostitution were strong and sometimes unbalanced. While pitying profoundly 'the poor girls' and detesting their seducers, she was inclined to regard all unorthodox forms of rescue work as exhibitionism or worse . . . and she sometimes thought that the 'Hallelujah lassies' were no better than they ought to be . . . Her real objection was to public revelations about immorality, between which and sensation mongering she saw no difference. 'There have been horrible things published and talked about of late, under the plea of virtue and humanity, which has and will do fearful harm.'

As the trial was coming to an end it dawned on Stead that Eliza's father had been so indifferent to her fate — save his one abortive journey to Loriol — that perhaps he was not her father after all. Stead consulted Mr. (later Sir) Charles Russell, counsel for Rebecca but, for reasons which must have seemed good to him, he was unwilling to take further action. Again for reasons which have never been made clear, Stead concurred. He needed only to have sent one of his

clerks to Somerset House, or asked Bramwell Booth for one
of his officers to call — and the truth would have been out.
The case for the prosecution would have collapsed beyond
repair. In her televised study of the trial, Alison Plowden
states that ten years passed before it was discovered that
Eliza was the illegitimate daughter of Mrs. Armstrong. So
Stead received a sentence of three months, Rebecca six
months, Jacques one month, and Madame Mourez six
months — but in her case with hard labour. She died in
prison. Bramwell Booth and Madam Combe were acquitted.

Even now Stead's friends still laboured on his behalf.
Judgment was given on November 10th, 1885, but by the
afternoon of Tuesday, December 22nd, a further petition
was laid on the floor of the Commons praying for the release
of W. T. Stead and Rebecca Jarrett — though without avail.

Both Mrs. Bramwell Booth and Mrs. Butler visited
Rebecca in prison, and Mrs. Booth was waiting at seven
o'clock in the morning to welcome her on her release. Under
another name she remained a good Salvationist until her
death in 1928. Stead offered to resign his editorship but this
was refused, and he laboured in such causes as lay closest
to his heart until his death when the *Titanic* sank in 1912.

There were those who openly declared that the Armstrong
case would crush The Salvation Army, and there were others
with whom the wish was father to the thought. But the end
aim was greater than any who laboured or suffered to secure
it. The age of consent was raised, and any who think it
should be lowered again should remember the shame from
which this country was once delivered.

5

The Burden of the Lord

As the name of Catherine Booth occurred in the previous
chapter even more than that of William, it is time to take
note of this marriage of true minds. High time, in fact —
for her life was to end even before his *In Darkest England
and the Way Out* was off the press.

Victorian society in Britain was fortunate to possess
several outstanding couples who were as much of one mind
in their private relationships as they were in their public
service. Samuel and Henrietta Barnett were one such pair;
George and Josephine Butler another; William and Catherine Booth yet another — and by no means the least in
that elect company. They set their contemporaries an example of personal religion without religiosity and of social
concern without sentimentality. If at times they differed in
opinion, their two hearts never ceased to beat as one.

Both William and Catherine had a mind of their own.
Both could feel deeply and speak forthrightly. If (as their
eldest son has written) his father could be irascible when
displeased, neither did his mother always suffer fools gladly.
At times she could wish that some of 'the dear Lord's idiot
children' (as she called them) had as much knowledge as
zeal. Catherine's Swedish biographer, Dr. Laura Petri, well
declared that 'the Army was started, not with one motor but
two.' If William acted with the directness of an old Testament prophet to whom the word of the Lord had come,
Catherine frequently supplied the rationale for his actions,
for both were animated by a truly biblical concern.

A biblical concern — be it noted, for it is beside the point to insist that neither of the two were students of economics. This was a blessing in disguise, else they could have been chained to Malthus on the right hand and Ricardo on the left. The one declared that the population would always increase faster than the means of subsistence, and therefore want and woe were the inescapable lot of many. Ricardo taught that the increase of wealth was best secured without any action by the state, so these were the law and prophets by which the inhuman exploitation of human beings which marked the Industrial Revolution was justified. As Wordsworth wrote: 'Gain (was) the master idol of the realm.' How far William Booth was from bowing the knee to this baal is seen by contrasting the Malthusian dictum that 'man has no claim of right to the smallest portion of food' with his own statement in *The Darkest England Gazette* of August 19th, 1893: 'It is beyond question the duty of society to supply the absolute necessities of existence to such of its members as are in danger of perishing from the want of them.'

With this principle in mind, William borrowed many of his facts and figures from his namesake, Charles Booth, and publicly acknowledged his indebtedness. But to neither William or Catherine was any human being a digit in an analytical survey. Their social concern did not arise from a study of blue books, but from their awareness of the sovereign rule of a living God and of His eternal love for His creatures. Woe unto the man who caused the least of them to stumble. 'Better for him that a millstone were hanged about his neck, and he cast into the sea.' With the inexorable passion of an Amos or a Micah they declared that the righteous God required men to behave righteously toward one another. Only the justice of God was not a demand for the uttermost farthing. Samuel Butler had the prophets on his side when he wrote that:

> . . . Justice, though she's painted blind,
> Is to the weaker side inclined.

Justice and mercy are not like oil and water which cannot mix, but are complementary parts of the divine righteousness. This is why the Scriptures declare God to be 'the helper of the fatherless', the deliverer of 'the needy . . . the poor also, and him that hath no helper.' This was why the prophets of the eighth century B.C. were markedly partial to those whom we euphemistically call 'the underprivileged.' God was both 'a righteous God and a Saviour', and therefore a man's treatment of his neighbour was to be marked by a like goodwill. This was why the provisions for fair dealing found, for example, in the book of Deuteronomy, far exceed any strict *quid pro quo*. The poor, the widow, the resident alien ('the stranger that is within thy gates') were to be treated mercifully because the Lord is plenteous in mercy. It was this divine pity which possessed William and Catherine. Economic theories change from generation to generation. What is vehemently urged today as serving the greatest good of the greatest number could be condemned out of hand tomorrow, just as some of yesterday's sovereign remedies have already been denounced today. But the compassion of God fails not, which is why, even in cold print, the addresses which Mrs. Booth gave in the autumn of 1884 in the Prince's Hall, Piccadilly, still burn with holy fire.

Few were the social evils which she did not challenge. Hear her, for example, on 'sweating':

As the stories come to me from Hackney Wick, Seven Dials, St. George's, the Borough . . . stories of destitution, sickness, sorrow and suffering no less than of sin and crime and shame, what can I say that will arouse God's professed people to some concern and care . . .?

(Here are) men and women nearly naked, children absolutely so, women who must not look up from their matchbox making at 2½d. per gross, or their shirt stitching at 3d. each, for fear of reducing their earnings by a half-penny, and thus robbing their children of an ounce of bread, or the rent of their wretched room of the last fraction which an inexorable (perhaps Christian?) landlord exacts.

Thousands of such wretched human beings, without a bed to lie on, without a fire to warm them, or sufficient food to keep body and soul together, are living in the greatest degradation and sin all over London, perhaps not two hundred yards from the very spot where we are assembled this afternoon, and yet who cares for them?

Or this on irresponsible luxury:

I concur in the denunciation of all these evils (i.e. drunkenness among the poor which leads to family quarrels and fighting and the break-up of homes). But what sort of taste is it which, in the presence of this state of things among the poor, spends not fourpence on a quart of beer, but four shillings — and double and treble that sum — on a single bottle of wine for the jovial entertainment of a few friends, and from twenty to forty pounds upon a dinner to be swallowed by a dozen or two of people?

I maintain that no splendid furniture, no well-trained and liveried servants, no costly pictures or display of finery or jewels, can redeem such a scene, viewed in the light of the teachings of Christ, from being called 'brutal' — and all the more brutal because delighted in by persons whose intelligence and knowledge of the world around them must make them fully aware of the good that might be done with the money which they lavish upon themselves.

Or this on commercialism run riot:

It is never convenient . . . to ask how Mr. Moneymaker gets the golden sovereigns or crisp notes which look so well in the collection. He may be the most accursed sweater who ever waxed fat on the murderous cheap needlework system, which is slowly destroying the bodies and ruining the souls of thousands of poor women ... He may keep scores of employees standing wearily sixteen hours per day behind the counter, across which they dare not speak the truth, and on salaries so small that all hope of marriage and home is denied them.

Or he may trade in some damning thing which robs men of all that is good in this world and all hope for the next .. such as intoxicating drink, but if you are simple enough to suppose that modern Christianity would object to him on account of any of those things ... how respectable Christians would open their eyes and, in fact, suspect that you had recently made your escape from some lunatic asylum and should be hastened back there as soon as possible.

Or on the housing shortage:

It is a shameful scandal for Christian landlords to keep their tenants in buildings unfit for dogs but, after all, not so much more shameful than the conduct of those who, although aroused to the condition of the masses, deliberately attempt their improvement on the same principles as if they were cattle, mainly by means of buildings which pay a liberal interest. No one could possibly be more thankful than I to see the compassion which of late has found such loud expression in words, embodied in some practical scheme for the provision of comfortable, wholesome houses for the poor, at such a rental as they could comfortably pay; but to provide this, with land under our present iniquitous system, will require a benevolence willing to 'lend, hoping for nothing again.'

Or this on blood sports:

Here is His Grace, the Duke of Rackrent, and the

Right Honourable Woman Seducer Fitz-Shameless, and the gallant Colonel Swearer, with half the aristocracy of the county, male and female, mounted on horses worth hundreds of pounds apiece, and which have been bred and trained at a cost of hundreds more — and what for? This splendid field is waiting while an animal is let loose from confinement and then permitted to fly from its strange surroundings.

Observe the delight of all the gentlemen and noble ladies when the whole pack of dogs is let loose in pursuit, and behold them in noble chase. The regiment of well mounted cavalry and the pack of hounds all charge at full gallop after the frightened creature. It will be a great disappointment if by any means it should escape, or be killed within as short a time as an hour . . .

Brutality! I tell you that, in my judgment at any rate, you can find nothing in the slums more utterly, more deliberately, or more savagely cruel than that.

After that no one is surprised that Catherine's eldest grand-daughter should refer to 'her fury at cruelty and injustice,' or that her eldest son should agree that 'she had many of the limitations which went with the Puritan temper in the middle of the nineteenth century' — as is illustrated by a further extract from one of her addresses. Taking up the charge that the Victorian poor 'breathed an atmosphere of moral pollution,' she retorted that:

. . . there is an atmosphere of moral pollution, not a whit less dangerous, and far more blameworthy, in different circles.

Is it not notorious that multitudes of people amongst what are called the higher classes deliberately denude themselves of ordinary clothing, and then go in a half-dressed condition, with every addition of ornament that can be conceived, to ensure that they shall be noticed and admired, to large places of public amusement? Is there not a growing disposition in Christian circles to look upon it as perfectly harmless for Christian families, including often those of ministers, to spend hours together, dressed in the way I have described, at parties, balls and other entertainments, frequently given within the precincts of some consecrated building, or in order to raise money for church purposes?

Now, I ask, how comes it to pass that the poor are spoken of as herding together without any regard for decency, under the circumstances of necessity which I have described, while the herding together of the well-to-do in this voluntary indecency, should be regarded with complacency and described as refined and genteel? That such is the judgment of modern Christendom can only be attributed to one fact — the power of the purse; and that the churches should in the main devote their attention to the well-to-do classes, while they regard the masses of the people as a kind of outside element, to be operated on by separate agencies such as a few missionaries and Bible-women is, I contend, a crying scandal to the Saviour's name.

Those who could not speak for themselves could be thankful that Catherine Booth dared to lift up her voice like a trumpet on their behalf, though even a noble indignation was not the only, nor the most frequently used, weapon in her armoury. Natural diffidence had long provided a natural restraint. While still at Gateshead she had received an invitation from the leaders' meeting to address a series of specially convened prayer meetings. 'Of course I declined,' she commented. 'I don't know what they can be thinking of!' In an obituary notice *The War Cry* for October 11th, 1890, noted that 'there was a time when she dared not speak in the presence of her husband. "If I but saw that nose, it was all up with me for that meeting." '

Moreover, the manner of her speaking won a hearing even from those who would otherwise have rejected her forceful argumentation. As a young student, Dr. J. C. Carlile, C.H. heard her preach at a Sunday morning meeting held in a room over a coffee bar in Whitechapel. 'This,' as he said in his autobiography, *My Life's Little Day*, 'was religion with the fragrance of flowers, the laughter of little children, and the common sense of a mature mind.' No woman who, however strong her convictions, was content only to denounce, would ever have been called — as she was by *The Daily Telegraph* on her death — 'the female Melanchthon of a Movement in which her husband was the Luther who fought the devil not only with prayer, but with rough and ready jokes.' For whatever vested evil might have been scorched by her burning words, her own heart could not have been more tender towards those who suffered because of that evil.

Back in her Gateshead days she had devoted two evenings a week to the systematic visitation of the dwellings which huddled around her husband's chapel. 'There was not a stick of furniture to be seen, nor anywhere to sit down,' she commented after trying to arrange what might hopefully have been called a house meeting. In another shanty she found a woman who had given birth to twins, with no one in the place to help her, lying on a collection of rags, a crust of bread and a lump of lard — the destitute's substitute for butter — beside her. As one woman concerned for another, Catherine Booth tidied up the mother and washed the babies as best she could, though facilities for doing so were virtually non-existent. But then, as W. T. Stead once remarked, no one had need of a step ladder to get within speaking distance of Catherine Booth.

Without doubt the slow but certain revolution in the social position of women in the second half of the nineteenth century was greatly aided by the simple fact that she lived in that age. As Florence Nightingale opened a closed door in nursing practice, and Josephine Butler in social concern, so did Catherine Booth in the service of the deprived and dispossessed. No longer need any woman keep silence

— not even in a church. The door which she helped to open
no man has been — or will be — able to shut. By the professional standards of C. P. Scott few undeserved bouquets
were ever offered but, on Catherine's death, *The Manchester
Guardian* said that 'she had probably done more in her own
person to establish the right of women to preach the gospel
than anyone who had ever lived.' And when it is remembered
what she meant by 'the gospel,' with its concern for the
well-being of the whole man in his spiritual and social
relationships alike, that was no small compliment.

It was in the spring of 1888 that Catherine knew that
time was running out for her. On June 21st of the same year
she delivered her last public address in the City Temple, and
shortly afterwards there appeared in *The War Cry* a pathetic
announcement asking any reader who knew of a genuine
cure for cancer to communicate with General Booth. There
may have been many replies — but no cure was forth-
coming, and the sufferer lingered until October 4th, 1890.
But neither weakness nor pain diminished her interest in the
proposals for social action which her husband was preparing.
He read passages to her in her bedroom. She answered with
her comments, and lived long enough to know that the final
draft of *In Darkest England and the Way Out* had been sent
to the printers.

At this time of day Catherine Booth needs no one either
to defend her evangelical heart or her social conscience.
They were inseparable parts of her love for God and man.
But perhaps the judgment of George Lansbury might not be
out of place. In his *Looking Backwards — and Forwards* he
said:

I, and my fellow Socialists, often criticised her and her
work. Looking back after these years I can see that we
were hopelessly wrong and she was right. We said that the
system was wrong, and that all the time it was manufac-
turing misery and wrecking human lives faster than ever
she could hope to mend them. This was absolutely true,

but we were doctrinaires all the same . . . The world went on despite our arguments and men did not control their passions — either their sexual passions or their passionate greed for money . . . Her speeches and appeals on behalf of the weak and fallen were among the finest pieces of simple, arresting oratory I ever heard.

It has rightly been said that Catherine Booth was not content to leave world affairs to secular leaders. She knew her Bible too well to forget the apostolic word: 'Do you not know that the saints are to manage the world?' (I Corinthians 6: 2, Moffatt).

6

Good Tidings to all People

Five years elapsed between the passing of the Criminal Law Amendment Act and the publication of *In Darkest England and the Way Out*. Far from the Eliza Armstrong story proving the ruin of The Salvation Army, the widespread publicity given to the Old Bailey trial meant that any girl in moral danger, or any woman anxious to change her way of life, now knew who were her true friends. Once more the wrath of man was turned to the praise of God.

Within two years four new reception centres for women were opened in London, in addition to others in Cardiff, Glasgow and Plymouth. A pilot maternity scheme was commenced in Hackney, and homes were provided elsewhere for mothers and babies. A monthly paper specialising in work for, by, and among women, called *The Deliverer* was launched in July 1889, and is still in circulation. Other women's homes were opened in Australia, Canada, Ceylon, France, New Zealand, South Africa, Sweden and the United States.

Meanwhile William Booth had continued to brood over the necessity for an all inclusive plan of social action which would deal not merely with individual cases of destitution, but with the needs of all who lived on or below the poverty line. In the climate of the times it was no use waiting for any government, whatever its political hue, to take the initiative. 'It rarely happens,' declared *The Times*, 'that in England any great scheme of comprehensive benevolence is initiated by the government which is only too happy to await the results of private enterprise and private experience.'

Spontaneous though sporadic attempts had been, and were being made to cope with specific areas of want. Nineteenth-century society believed in societies. The most enduring and the most effective of them were undoubtedly linked with the Christian church — either by virtue of their administrative structure, or the personal faith of their respective founders, or both. They ranged from the 'Ladies' Institution for Females of Weak Intellect' to the 'Committee for the Nightly Shelter of the Homeless Poor'. 'And yet — wrote William Booth in his preface to *In Darkest England* — 'all through my career I have keenly felt the remedial measures enunciated in Christian programmes and ordinarily employed by Christian philanthropy to be lamentably inadequate for any effectual dealing with the despairing miseries of these outcast classes . . . At last,' he added, 'I may be going to see my longings to help the workless realised.' So with the help of W. T. Stead, together with the results of Charles Booth's researches, plus the case histories supplied by officers who had learned the facts of life from first-hand experience, *In Darkest England and the Way Out* (pp. 336, 3s. 6d.) appeared on October 20th, 1890, six days after Catherine Booth had been buried in Abney Park.

Charles Booth had already reached the conclusion that one-third of the population of London lived on or below the poverty level. This third included 'the poor' whose weekly income ranged from 18s. to 21s., and 'the very poor' whose weekly income was even less. There were variations in the poverty level even in different parts of the East End, but the generally accepted estimate was that those above and below the poverty line were as 65: 35.

Accepting these figures, and working on them even more cautiously than the scrupulously careful Charles, William arrived at a figure of three million persons as constituting the country's 'submerged tenth'. Joseph Chamberlain had stated that 'a population equal to that of the metropolis' — i.e. between four and five million — were 'constantly in a state of abject destitution', so William Booth was not exaggerating.

Agree or disagree with him — for few could remain neutral, much less indifferent, in his company — William Booth had at least done his homework. The principles on which he proposed to work were set out for all to read, as were the methods he intended to employ. As likely as not the very first of his seven principles (detailed below) must have been a stone of stumbling to all but the most committed of Christian believers, and even some of them may have questioned whether he was not relying too heavily upon the impalpable factor of divine grace.

Two questions arose. Was it not going beyond the limits of Christian action to relate Christian truth to the admittedly distressing personal consequences of an impersonal economic order? Should not commercial considerations rule the life that now is, leaving spiritual considerations for the life that is to come? Prime Minister Melbourne was not long dead who held that things had come to a pretty pass when religion was allowed to interfere with a man's personal affairs.

In the second place, was not the efficacy of divine grace dependent upon the free consent of sinful man? All true! No one needed to tell William Booth that he had to reckon with that deadweight of individual and collective egoism for which the theological name is original sin. It might have seemed to many to be the height of folly to propose any scheme of social redemption which relied in the least upon such a non-economic factor as the Christian doctrine of the grace of God. But William Booth knew that it would have been even greater folly to have attempted any such scheme without it.

Undeterred, he set out his seven principles of action which may be paraphrased as saying that:

1. Where character weaknesses were the cause of a man's failure, then his character must be cleansed and

strengthened. He needed to know the power of Christian conversion.

2. Where a man's circumstances were the cause of his failure, then his circumstances must be changed — an acknowledgment that though a man's environment does not necessarily determine his conduct, it can condition it.

3. Any such corrective action must be adequate to cope with one, or both, of the above evils.

4. In addition, such remedial action must be immediately practicable; (5) lasting in its results; (6) without injurious side-effects and (7) while helping one man would not harm his neighbour.

In an age where it was a prime article of faith that a government, while maintaining law and order, should not interfere with the free play of economic forces, William Booth brought forward his three tier remedy commencing with what he called 'the city colony'. This was his name for what now might be described as a primary rehabilitation centre where the immediate physical needs of applicants might be met, temporary work provided, and training given which would either facilitate their return to normal employment, or enable them to benefit from the second stage of the scheme — the farm colony. (Here was a forerunner of the current re-training schemes for the unemployed in the United Kingdom.)

As the exodus from the country to the city had been a contributory cause to the number of men out of work, William Booth proposed to reverse that trend by the establishment of training farms where colonists would receive a thorough grounding in such agricultural skills as would enable them either to be received into private employment, or find work on one of the several co-operative farms which he proposed to establish.

Finally, overseas colonies would be set up in, for example, Australia, Canada or southern Africa where land, available in abundance, was capable of supporting as many migrants as could be transferred in the foreseeable future.

Once again, though William Booth was not an economist in the academic sense, his schemes were marked by economic wisdom. In addition, he possessed what some professional economists of his day lacked — a Christian insight into the worth of man as man. If he fully recognised the duty of the individual to the community, he also brought into the open the duty of the community to the individual — and this he embodied in his memorable 'cab horse charter.'

He may have owed the germ of the phrase to Carlyle who earlier had pointed out that 'there are not many horses in England, able and willing to work, which have not due food and lodging.' In a parable from the London streets William Booth drew attention to the fact that every cab horse in the city had shelter for the night, food for its stomach, and work by which to earn its keep. It profited the owner to see that his animal was so treated. 'How much then is a man better than a sheep?' asked Jesus. Or a horse, His Salvationist disciple added.

Whatever William Booth's sources, the initial impact of *In Darkest England and the Way Out* was phenomenal. Some denigrators sought to shift the credit for this to 'the energetic prose which W. T. Stead so skilfully employed', albeit — added St. John Ervine in *God's Soldier* — from Booth's 'elaborate notes.' At this time of day it is impossible to say where one man's work ended and the other began. William Booth openly avowed the 'valuable literary help (received) from a friend of the poor.' Stead's own version of the part he played appeared in *The Star* for January 2nd, 1891. He wrote:

General Booth naturally and properly called upon all those under his command to render whatever assistance they could towards making the new departure a success. That is obvious from the structure and nature of the book. It is composed largely of reports from officers in the field . . .

When he got these reports he set to work writing his book. At that time Mrs. Booth was dying, but by the aid of diligent dictating and laborious writing he succeeded in preparing a book which in its rough state was about twice or thrice the size of *In Darkest England* . . .

It was then that the General asked me to find him a literary hack who would help him to lick this huge and growing mass of material into shape. I volunteered to hack . . . It is his scheme if ever a scheme was any man's, and although many were glad to help, the sole responsibility and the dominating mind were his and his alone.

The public response exceeded all expectations. Here was a best seller before the word had been coined. A first edition of 10,000 was sold out on the day of publication, and within a year *The War Cry* was advertising a fifth edition — bringing the total sales up to 200,000.

The scheme did not lack a varied army of well wishers. The Prince of Wales who, disguised as a sanitary inspector, had already visited the slums of St. Pancras, wrote expressing his personal interest. Keir Hardie, then M.P. for West Ham, described the proposals as 'giving an important object lesson in what could be accomplished if the state would act with force and energy.' 'I start,' said Campbell Bannerman, 'with a firm prejudice in favour of William Booth, his powers and his methods.' The observations of Sir John Gorst, Q.C., M.P., read as if he were commending the brain child of one of the most far-sighted administrators of the day. 'The unemployed,' he wrote, 'is taken away from the town where he competes with a congested mass of workers, too numerous for existing employment opportunities, and brought back to the land, where he produces more than he consumes, where his labour enriches the nation without lessening the earnings of his fellow workmen.'

There was notable — though by no means unanimous — support from the press. One instance was that of *The Star* which commented that —

... today, the General holds the field, and the three hundred pages of *In Darkest England and the Way Out*, with its nervous, graceful and suggestive style, will be perused with a feeling akin to that which stirred the readers of *Alton Locke* and the hearers of some thunderous preachment of a Jerome or Chrysostom. For The Salvation Army has a right to speak in this matter. It is not a mere offshoot of aristocratic or middle class sentiment. It comes from the people.

Said the *Daily Telegraph*:

We hope that General Booth's great experiment ... will have a good start, fair play and eventual success. It certainly does not bear the common stamp of the many philanthropic undertakings which in London and other great cities casually assist and generally demoralise the poor. The General applies to social improvement the principles he has already used in his religious reformation.

The *Daily Graphic* wrote that —

General Booth's title to an exceptionally attentive hearing is twofold. The Salvation Army has worked more consistently, and on a larger scale, in darkest England than any other organisation of mercy ... It gains power for further efforts by using its proselytes of the slums to approach the shy ferocity of the hardened and abandoned ... The General's book may be commended both to those who are interested in the fate of their fellow men and those who are not.

Many churchmen were among the warmest supporters of the scheme. Cardinal Manning lined himself alongside William Booth by saying that 'I have already sufficient knowledge of its contents to say at once how fully it commands my sympathy.' At the other end of the ecclesiastical spectrum R. W. Dale devoted a Sunday morning at Carr's

Lane to a study of the book. Among other church leaders who urged that the proposals contained therein 'should have a fair and adequate trial' were John Clifford, Grattan Guinness, John McNeil, Joseph Parker and Alexander Whyte. When T. H. Huxley — of whom more anon — attacked the scheme in a series of letters to *The Times*, Archdeacon Farrar answered him seriatim in *The Daily Graphic*. Perhaps the most moving of all comments were those of Francis Thompson who was asked by Wilfrid Meynell to review the book.

> I had knowledge more intimate than most men of this life which is not a life; to which food is as the fuel of hunger; sleep, our common sleep, precious, costly and fallible, as water in the wilderness; in which men rob and women vend themselves; because I have such knowledge, I read with painful sympathy the book *In Darkest England* just put forward by a singular personality. I rise from the reading of it with a strong impression that here is at last a man who has formulated a comprehensive scheme, and has dared to take upon himself its execution . . .
>
> In God's name, give him the contract! And, except in God's name, it were wanton to try it.

Wanton indeed! For one of the unwelcome results of the astounding reception of *In Darkest England* was that the malicious or the ill-informed — and these were not just the ignorant — assumed, tongue in cheek, that the millennium was about to dawn. The London *Sun* commented that 'General Booth was going to take care of the unemployed and down-trodden and criminal of the whole country, and was backed by a fabulous sum.' Another yarn was that General Booth had declared that, if his scheme was adopted, in five years there would not be a pauper left in London. By contrast, *The Methodist Times* thought that he had bitten off more than he could chew. 'Much of the best life and energy of The Salvation Army,' so ran an editorial, 'will be drained away from the spiritual sphere and devoted to social enterprises.'

William Booth and his helpers needed neither praise nor blame to help them realise the weight of the burden they had voluntarily shouldered. The total abolition of destitution was beyond their power. What private individual or institution — and the Army, of all voluntary societies, had no unlimited reserves either of manpower or money — could put to rights a state so inherently conservative in its ways as Victorian Britain?

'I see no way out of this present depression,' wrote Elijah Cadman who, at the beginning of 1891, took over the leadership of what was then known as the Social Reform Wing when Frank Smith resigned, 'unless the government is prepared to take action . . . The ruling powers are, as a rule, intensely awake to the duty of protecting property and capital in every shape and form, but they perpetually fail to help and protect the helpless. And what is the inevitable result? The surplus workers — if I may so call them — are left to fester in poverty until they become a running sore.'

But Christian initiative was not to be halted because Westminster slumbered, and so William Booth pursued his self-appointed task of arousing the country to the unnecessary poverty that existed in the midst of plenty, and of providing for its victims. He asked for £100,000 to set his plan in motion. By modern standards, this was peanuts. Like Clive, he could have stood astonished at his own moderation. He also asked for another £30,000 annually to sustain, and develop, the work when commenced.

In the event £102,559 1s. 2d. was subscribed by January, 1891. On the evening of the 30th, at a public meeting of thanksgiving in the St. James Hall, William Booth signed the 'Darkest England' Trust Deed by which he became legal trustee of the fund, guaranteeing the security of all the properties listed under this heading. He further pledged that all such assets would be maintained separately from other Salvation Army funds, and agreed that any breach of such trust would lay him open to action by the Attorney General.

It was in respect of the annual maintenance of the scheme that the response proved as disappointing as the original appeal had been encouraging. When William Booth reported on the progress of the social work at a crowded Queen's Hall meeting on May 20th, 1895, he had to announce that 'during the first year or two not much more than £3,000' — not the £30,000 for which he had asked — 'had been subscribed. And, apart from what the Army was providing little more was coming in at the present moment.'

This was a serious setback, but undismayed and with characteristic generosity, he turned over the profit of £7,383 on the sale of *In Darkest England* to the scheme itself. But even so disinterested a gesture was not enough to avert the storm of criticism which was about to break over his head.

7

For my Love they are my Adversaries

Hostile comment on the *Darkest England* scheme could be divided into three parts. There was no such widespread need as William Booth had described. Or, if there was, current public relief, when properly administered, was adequate. This being so, the man was only seeking notoriety or money — possibly both — for himself.

The substance of the first charge was that William Booth had invented a dragon so that he might pose as St. George. This was the attitude of the then Lord Mayor of London, Sir David Evans. As head of the city corporation he had been asked whether there were any empty buildings which could be placed at the disposal of The Salvation Army to shelter those who were sleeping out all night — for example, on Blackfriars Bridge. A head count undertaken by Salvation Army officers of those who were sleeping rough in this one area totalled 164.

The official answer was that this could not possibly be correct because the police had 'strict orders . . . that no one was allowed to remain all night on any of the bridges within the jurisdiction of the city authorities, and during the recent inclement weather special instructions had been issued on the subject to prevent people — apparently homeless — from loitering or falling asleep.' With this statement the Lord Mayor associated himself, adding that no exceptional distress existed in London.

For those who can interpret officialese, the operative word in this bland assertion was 'exceptional'. The prevailing distress was in the normal order of things. What late night owls saw on the Thames bridges, and what Gustave Doré had portrayed more than once in his sketches of London life, was not abnormal. By the Lord Mayor's crooked logic, no action needed to be taken about it.

Near neighbour to this twisted outlook was the attitude of those who, while admitting that there were human needs which called for attention, maintained that existing remedies were adequate. 'In certain circles,' wrote William Booth, 'one is not only advised that the existing state of things is inevitable, but is assured that no further machinery is necessary to deal with it. All that is needed in this direction is already in working order, and to create any further machinery, or to spend any more money, will do more harm than good.'

But *In Darkest England* helped to destroy that comfortable illusion wherever it still existed. Legally, the state accepted responsibility for providing food and shelter for every destitute man. But such relief was made all but impossible by the imposition of impossible conditions, and William Booth spelled these out in studiously moderate language. There was no need for him to rant. The facts themselves were grievous enough. And William the prophet — like one of his Old Testament forbears — wrote them so plainly that they could be read at a glance.

No Englishman can come upon the rates so long as he has anything whatever left to call his own. When long continued destitution has reached its bitter end, when piece by piece every article of domestic furniture has been sold or pawned, when all efforts to procure employment have failed, and when you have nothing left except the clothes in which you stand, then you can present yourself before the relieving officer and secure your lodging in the workhouse.

If, however, you have not sunk to such despair as to to be willing to barter your liberty for the sake of food, clothing and shelter ... but are only temporarily out of employment, then you go to the casual ward. There you are taken in and provided for on the principle of making it as disagreeable as possible for yourself, in order to deter you from again accepting the hospitality of the rates ... Under existing regulations, if you are compelled to seek refuge in a casual ward on a Monday evening, you must stay there until Wednesday morning.

The work given is the same as that given to felons in gaol, oakum picking and stone breaking ... Four pounds of oakum is more than the amount demanded from a criminal ... The stone breaking test is monstrous. Half a ton of stone from any man in return for partially supplying the cravings of hunger is an outrage which, if we read of it as occurring in Russia or Siberia, would find Exeter Hall crowded with an indignant audience and Hyde Park filled with strong oratory ... If the task is not done, the alternative is the magistrate and the gaol.

Chapter and verse could be given many times over the the last sentence. *The Social Gazette* for August 20th, 1898, reported that James Lewis, labourer, was charged with failing to break seven cwt. of stone in return for food and shelter in the casual ward of the Stroud workhouse, and was sentenced to fourteen days' imprisonment with hard labour.

Workhouse discipline itself could be as merciless. On December 17th, 1898, the *Gazette* noted that, at the Worship Street (London) police court, a female pauper who left the workhouse dinner table before the appointed time because her suet pudding was uneatable, was given fourteen days' hard labour for insubordination.

Prison was preferable to the 'spike'. About the same time the same Army paper reported that a Michael Mainwaring, admitted to the casual ward, was set to stone breaking, but the customary inspection showed that he had failed to fulfil his appointed task. Brought before a magistrate and sentenced to fourteen days' hard labour, Mainwaring replied fervently: 'Thank you, sir.'

Nor was this sham bravado. There was little to choose between oakum picking and stone breaking. Oakum was thick old rope, cut into lengths, stiff with tar and exposure to the weather, which had to be unravelled to the consistency of fluff. The process inevitably produced an unbearable assortment of sores, though old hands knew how to put the iron heel tip of a navvy's boot to good use. Of course, all money, tobacco, matches and the like were taken from their owner on entering. The hardened dosser would bury his personal possessions under a hedge, or other suitable hiding place, before knocking at the door. To be destitute was to be treated like a criminal — though without benefit of court proceedings.

Other candid friends chided William Booth that, in embracing the cause of the poor, he had failed to acknowledge the labours of those who were in the field before him, and who now were alongside him. This was the reproach of Lady Jeune. 'As regards every other charitable enterprise,' she wrote, 'General Booth is silent. His book, from beginning to end, is a tacit indictment of the Church of England and the Nonconformists ... It would have been better policy on his part to have admitted what is being done by the great religious bodies.'

In defence, the appendices to *In Darkest England* should be noted though it is correct that, in his own forthright way, William Booth pulled no punches in describing 'the remedial measures enunciated in Christian programmes ... (as) lamentably inadequate.' This was true enough, if less than tactful, but mild in an age when abrasive exchanges were common even between religious leaders. Lord Shaftesbury's favourite adjective for Bishop Wilberforce was 'satanical.' Gladstone was 'low, tortuous and timid.' Booth's doings were 'anti-Christian ... an expression as offensive as any that ever disgraced the wildest fanaticism.' It is greatly to the credit of William and Catherine that they never replied in kind, and even if William Booth did not offer the other cheek to Huxley, he kept his hands at his sides.

Thomas Henry Huxley was an opponent of the *Darkest England* scheme who, by reason of his scientific eminence, was a foe to be reckoned with. He was a Fellow of the Royal Society, had been a President of the British Association, and was almost an obligatory choice when any of the numerous Royal Commissions was being set up. As might be expected, he was one of the most articulate of men though, in the paper war which he waged against William Booth in the columns of *The Times*, his zeal finally outran his judgment.

A collection of his letters, published by Macmillans under the title of *Social Diseases and Worse Remedies* will show that he began temperately enough, but argument gave way to vituperation when he stigmatised 'Mr. Booth's system . . . as autocratic socialism, masked by its theological exterior.' Remembering that, in the nineteenth century, the word 'socialism' carried in some minds the same horrific overtones as are associated today with the word 'communism', the charge throws more light on the mental state of Huxley than the compassionate intentions of William Booth. When later Ben Tillett was discovered to approve of the social schemes of The Salvation Army, Mr. Huxley felt that his worst fears were about to be realised.

Yielding to an apprehensive imagination, he drew a picture of a General who, in days to come, would have '100,000 officers' pledged to do his bidding, with the absolute control of 'eight or ten millions sterling of capital, and as many of income, with barracks in every town and estates scattered throughout the country' holding the nation to ransom. William Booth must surely have smiled wryly on reading this. Millions in the plural. 'O that I had!' He had asked only for one-tenth of one million for the dream of his heart.

But Huxley was not to be stayed. 'Harlotry and

intemperance are sore evils' (he went on) 'and starvation is hard to bear, or even to know of, but . . . it is a greater evil to have the intellect of a nation put down by organised fanaticism; to see its political and industrial affairs at the mercy of a despot whose chief thought is to make that fanaticism prevail . . . But that is the end to which, in my opinion, all such organisations as that to which kindly people, who do not look to the consequences of their acts, are now giving their thousands, inevitably tend.' There was much more in the same vein, and when Huxley heard that a girl who had been seduced had been helped by the Army to trace the man involved and to bring him to book, he denounced William Booth's action 'as immoral as, I hope, it is illegal', and compared The Salvation Army to the Sicilian Mafia.

Such immoderate language was self-defeating. Cardinal Manning wrote that he had not the patience left to read Huxley's diatribes. All the same, he was not without his allies — notably the leaders of the Charity Organisation Society who saw in William Booth a threat to their place and their power. It was expedient that he should be put down. So 'Booth's pretentious plan' was written off as 'hopelessly sentimental, and its direction irresponsible and autocratic'. He was only tempting men to beg with his cheap refuges and free meals.

C. S. Loch joined Huxley in denouncing William Booth and all his works in *The Times*, and this letter was later expanded into a book which included papers by Bernard Bosanquet and Canon Philip Dwyer to the effect that existing agencies made superfluous any further private social schemes. One of their more enthusiastic supporters called for the revival of a statute dating from the reign of Henry VIII so that all idle and worthless vagabonds attracted to the nation's capital by the lure of gratuitous food and shelter might be legally expelled. Octavia Hill joined in the chorus when, appearing before a Royal Commission which sat in 1893/94, she stigmatised *In Darkest England* as 'the most gigantic scheme of inadequate relief ever devised by a human being.'

Hard words — but harder still to bear were the attacks upon William Booth's personal honesty. These he felt deeply and, as he wrote in *The War Cry* for August 6th, 1892, 'My social work has been attacked with such ... misrepresentation and open slander as ... no other Christian leader has been called upon to suffer for the last hundred years ... I have been charged with using the money given for the poor for my own family ... The accounts of the social scheme, it has been alleged, are imperfectly kept ... and the whole of our financial statements are unreliable.'

These allegations were all the more vexatious because it was still in living memory that a similar charge had been made against T. J. Barnardo and his 'East End Juvenile Mission for the care of Friendless and Destitute Children.' The Charity Organisation Society had moved in to mount its own committee of investigation into Barnardo's finances, though this was rejected by his trustees on the ground that they had already set up their own court of enquiry. Nevertheless the C.O.S. persisted and, though Barnardo was cleared of all intentional malpractice, it had to be admitted that he had lacked an adequate accounting system.

When therefore the correspondence columns of *The Times* carried a suggestion that William Booth should agree to an enquiry into the *Darkest England* scheme by a committee in whom the general public could have the fullest confidence, he agreed without demur. He was out of the country at the time, but at once instructed the Chief of the Staff, his eldest son, Bramwell Booth, to accept the proposal. He knew in advance that he had nothing to fear. Certified accounts had been published annually since 1867 — and the practice continues to this day.

Six public figures agreed so to serve — Sir Henry (afterwards Lord) James as chairman, the Earl of Onslow, Mr. Walter (afterwards Lord) Long, Mr. Sydney Buxton, M.P. (who later resigned on the death of his wife) and Mr. Edwin

Waterhouse, with Mr. C. E. Hobhouse as honorary secretary. Eighteen meetings were held, thirty witnesses were
heard — and these included, as the final report stated,
'those who have preferred charges against, or have adversely
criticised, the administration of the *Darkest England* funds
and institutions.' William Booth had given in advance an
undertaking that no legal action would be taken against
anyone who testified before the committee, whose terms of
reference read:

(1) Have the monies collected by means of the Appeal
made to the public in *In Darkest England and the Way
Out* been devoted to the objects and expended by the
methods set out in that Appeal, and to — and in — no
other?

(2) Have the methods employed in the expenditure of
such monies been, and are they, of a businesslike, econ-
omical and prudent character, and have the accounts of
such expenditure been kept in a proper and clear manner?

(3) Is the property, both real and personal, and are the
monies resulting from the above Appeal, now so vested
that they cannot be applied to any purposes other than
those set out in *The Darkest England*, and what safeguards
exist to prevent the misapplication of such property and
money, either now or after the death of Mr. Booth?

The members of the Committee went through the whole
of the Army's social services with a fine tooth comb. Their
report, dated December 2nd, 1892, ran to sixty-nine pages.
It covered virtually every detail of the *Darkest England*
scheme down to the prices charged at the food depots,
among which were listed nine items at a half-penny each.
The President of the Institute of Chartered Accountants
gave personal attention to the accounts and declared that
the books, kept on the double entry system, were regularly
audited by a competent firm from his own profession. A

large number of payments were compared with the associated vouchers and found to be in order.

Dealing with the aspersions that William Booth was lining his own pockets with the pennies of the poor, the members of the Committee declared that they had been careful to inquire — '. . . whether Mr. Booth or any of his family had drawn any sums for their personal use therefrom. No such expenditure appears to have been incurred. There is no reason to think that Mr. Booth or any member of his family derive, or ever have derived, benefit of any kind from any of the properties or money raised for the *Darkest England* scheme.'

The Committee had one reservation only — and this had to do not with William Booth but with the possible misapplication of funds by any of his successors. Any opening for such malpractice was effectively closed by the setting up of a Custodian Trustee Company under The Salvation Army Act of 1931.

Public opinion was all but unanimous in welcoming the report. The *Daily Telegraph* said that Lord Onslow's committee acquitted the General of any but the most disinterested aims. 'Mr. Booth vindicated' ran a heading in the *Morning Leader*. The *Daily News* declared that the report would be accepted as conclusive; the *Daily Chronicle* that it cleared the General. *The Times* was more grudging. William Booth was relieved of 'some of the graver charges made against his administration' but 'the investigations (were confined) to answering three questions and no other.' So indirectly the Committee was faulted for doing what it was asked to do — no more but no less. It is hard to please some of the people for even some of the time.

While William Booth's troubles were by no means over, his good faith was now established beyond serious question. Huxley died in 1895 and the attacks on the Army lost their virulence, though the General himself continued to be reproached by some for his a-political attitude, the Charity Organisation Society persisted in its hostility, and lone rangers like Jack London loosed off an occasional fusillade. But the man whose giant stature made him so conspicuous a target for his critics emerged even greater still when the sound and fury had died away.

8

Publish and Conceal Not

Vindicated by the Onslow Committee, William Booth pursued his twofold task of exposing the unacceptable face of Victorian poverty, and then putting into practice his published remedies. The first was no less important than the second, though in neither was he alone. James Greenwood, George R. Sims and Andrew Mearns — to name only three — anticipated him in print, though it is fair to say that none of them uncovered the facts of destitution so comprehensively, or offered remedial measures in such detail, as he did.

Even Charles Booth, in his compendious seventeen volumes on the *Life and Labour of the People of London* — only the first of which preceded the appearance of *In Darkest England* — was reluctant to propose any remedies for the ills he had so painstakingly analysed. Artists and writers — from home and abroad — had held up their several mirrors to various running sores in the body economic. Christian reformers — including William and Catherine Booth — had not been slow to lift up their voice with strength over wrongs unredressed, but on July 1st, 1893, William made himself a new and powerful ally. He added to his list of weekly papers — the best-known of which was *The War Cry* which first appeared at the close of 1879 — *The Darkest England Gazette*. This carried twelve pages and sold at one penny, but within a year the name was changed to *The Social Gazette*, the format to four pages measuring 23 ins. by 16 ins. and, after eighteen months, the price was reduced to one half-penny. The opening leader after the change of name ran:

We shall continue to voice, accurately and faithfully, the agony, suffering and sorrows of the poor; the failures, mistakes and misfortunes of the weak; the misery, wretchedness and crime of the vicious ... Side by side ... we shall show a way of escape from the pinch of poverty and the power of sin ... The haves must render succour to the have-nots.

As with its sister papers there was no supporting revenue from commercial advertising — which was just as well, for abuses in the field of child labour, or sweated labour, or casual labour, were unfailingly noted by its exploring eye. This was investigative reporting before the phrase had become commonplace. The circulation rose to 89,500 weekly, and its zeal did not flag until its demise in 1916, by which time the first hesitant steps had been taken in the United Kingdom towards the modern welfare state.

Take, for example, the scandal of home industries which led to the exploitation of unfortunate children by their equally unfortunate parents, driven to this extremity because of their own low wages or loss of employment.

Work would be brought from the factory to the home, completed there overnight, and returned to the factory in the morning. As an illustration, the finishing off of ladies' belts, made mostly of strong elastic to which buckle, clasp and slide had to be sewn, was paid at the rate of five farthings per dozen. A mother, or elder sister, after working a ten hour day, would bring home twelve dozen belts to be finished overnight. In this particular instance another family occupied each of the three other rooms in the house, and one child from each would be enlisted for the evening's work. This would include an older girl who had already done a day's work, another somewhat younger who had been helping to make match boxes in her own home, another two — younger still — who between school hours had been looking after the smallest of the children, or else carrying to a nearby tailor pairs of trousers which her mother had been finishing off. Supervised by the oldest of their number, the group of five fell to work and by half-past ten had finished the gross of belts for which the payment was fifteenpence, or three pence per person.

Another home industry in which children shared was artificial flower making. A middleman would pay fifteen pence per gross for primulas; eighteen pence a gross for cornflowers; half a crown a gross for roses, but only three halfpence a gross for violets. Three gross of roses could be completed in a day of fourteen hours for which the reward would be 7s. 6d. — but for no worker was it roses, roses all the way. There was always half a gross of primulas, or of violets, to go with the larger flowers. And if it be asked why any family should choose so to slave, the answer was that necessity knew no law. If a husband was out of work, or ill, or idle, the poor law was no adequate alternative.

Another home industry was sack making — as a Salvation Army eye-witness reported in *The Social Gazette* for February 17th, 1900.

After five o'clock every afternoon from spring to autumn, children may be seen in front of almost every house binding the edges of the sacks together with coarse twine, which they push through the rough jute with a thick needle. One end of the sacking is fixed to a hook in the wall and the child, holding the material tightly stretched, sews the two sides and the bottom together, and hems the top.

Thus, in addition to the force required to push the needle through the jute, and of drawing each individual stitch as tightly as possible, there is the constant strain of keeping the two edges of the sacking even by pulling against the hook. The least wrinkle when the sack is completed causes it to be condemned, and it has to be picked to pieces and sewn up all over again. The price paid is sixpence for two dozen sacks, or a farthing for a single sack, with the sewer providing his/her own needles and twine.

Paper bag making at home yielded the unbelievable return of three farthings per gross large brown bags, and three half-pence per thousand for small sweet bags. Before leaving for school the boy in the family would be sent to the factory for the allotted supply of paper, which the mother would cut into strips of the required size. One child would fold these; another would flick on the paste; a third would count and stack the finished bags. As likely as not a school inspector might call and find the children gainfully employed, but the fierce logic of the harassed mother was that if her children did not help her both she and they would starve. And if they starved, what use was schooling?

Box making was yet another such occupation — either cardboard boxes or match boxes. The former were mainly factory made, but the low wages rate made the additional income from home work not just desirable but essential. But match box making took up most of the time, and a contemporary *Punch* cartoon supported the on-the-spot enquiries of *The Social Gazette*. At the door of a garret in 'Mammon's Rents' stood the rent collector on his weekly call while the husband sat on the only chair with his head in his hands, his wife leaned helplessly against the mantelpiece, and four ragged children looked miserably around the chilly room. Above the fireless grate read a notice: 'Match boxes — 2¼d. per gross.' *The Social Gazette* added the information that the matchbox maker had to provide his own paste.

At the beginning of the present century The Salvation Army carried out its own independent — and highly ingenious — enquiry into the lot of the casual worker who might be a cab runner, a 'totter', a sandwich board carrier, or a balloon seller — like John Galsworthy's Tony Bicket. Charles Booth described street selling as the last resource of the old and broken-down, so it required an officer of some *nous* to dress himself up as a casual and live on his estimated takings of sixpence a day. His varying fortunes were meticulously chronicled in the ever watchful *Social Gazette*.

Embracing the vocation of a crossing sweeper, the new-

comer's first task was to buy himself a secondhand broom —
which he did for three halfpence at a back store near
Charing Cross.

Next came the choice of a pitch. It was a good afternoon
for his self-embraced calling — plenty of slush about — but
the apprentice sweeper had to abandon his first site at the
behest of a vigilant constable. He suffered a similar fate with
his second choice but, third time lucky, he was left in peace
and cleared a crossing which had to be reswept at intervals
as passing traffic bespattered it with mud. After forty
minutes he earned his first penny.

As time wore on a multitude of homegoers used the
crossing, but none recognised its maker until a carman's
boy hurriedly slipped a slice of bread, wrapped in newspaper, into his hand. Later on a mother sent her young
daughter back to him with a penny, and then an elegant
young thing, to whom he had tipped his hat, rewarded him
with three halfpence. Soon after six o'clock an old gentle-
man, as kind as he was portly, gave him sixpence, and by
the time he knocked off at eight o'clock in the evening, he
had earned 1s. 8d.

He had to hurry now to resell the broom to its original
owner for a penny, and then on to Blackfriars, for the Army
shelter there soon filled up. However he was in time to pay
twopence for a bunk, another penny for hot soup and a
chunk of bread, hot water in the ablutions was free — and
so to bed. A great sleep descended upon the open dormitory
when lights were lowered at ten o'clock. In the morning a
generous mug of tea and two slices of bread and marmalade
cost a penny, leaving more than enough for a midday meal
as he said, incognito, in an obscure corner in the Whitechapel shelter where he enjoyed a plate of meat, potatoes
and haricot beans for twopence.

In the afternoon he tried newsvending. The four o'clock
edition was hot off the press, and the new arrival purchased
a half-quire, thirteen copies, for 3½d. If he sold out, he would
be threepence to the good.

With a contents bill in his hand and his papers over his arm, he had hardly taken up his station on the kerbside when an aggressive stranger enquired in colourful language what he was doing there. The natural reply as to whether the questioner owned the Strand was answered by a quick but vicious punch in the ribs. With as dignified an air as possible the unwitting intruder moved to the opposite side of the road only to meet an equally hostile reception. 'My pitch for twenty yards over here.' The inexperienced one moved on again and had to try several other stands before he found rest for the soles of his feet.

Meanwhile the value of the four o'clock edition was speedily declining, and his three remaining copies would be obsolete when the five o'clock came out. However, he took another half-quire of the later edition, returned his unsold copies of the earlier, and by seven o'clock had sold another nine, making a total profit of 4½d. As the late night extra was now being hawked he retired from the scene, relying on his profit from the previous day to provide him with bed and breakfast as well as his midday meal on the morrow.

The self-appointed casual was even less fortunate on the morrow. He invested fivepence in a dozen penny boxes of wax lights, but by eight o'clock in the evening had sold only six. 'Enough to pluck the heart out of any white man,' was his comment. Still, he had enough in reserve to buy himself some supper (Irish stew, 1d.) bed (2d.), and breakfast (bloater, ½d., tea, ½d. and bread, ½d.), and feeling that he might do better were he more venturesome, decided next day to enter the hot potato business. A shelter acquaintance advised him on the techniques of his new calling and he borrowed, free of interest, the capital sum of 3s., which he expended as follows:

Hire of potato can, barrow and salt castor	1s. 0d.
Supply of coke	6d.
Supply of potatoes	1s. 6d.

Possible venues were considered. South London was ruled out. A man had to look tough and be tough as well to venture as far as the Elephant. The West End was rejected for the opposite reason. King's Cross seemed to provide the happy medium. The trade demanded a certain expertise. The fire must be maintained at a smokeless red glow. Acute judgment was needed to decide when to transfer potatoes from the lower to the upper drawer.

Sales were slow in the early evening but quickened as midnight approached, but by 1.30 a.m. it was no longer worth continuing, though the takings totalled but 2s. 8d. — a net loss of fourpence on the investment. By the time the barrow, potato can and salt castor had been returned to the hirer all the night refuges had closed their doors, and the quondam hot potato merchant had to wait until the Army shelter in Charles Street opened at five o'clock to allow early risers to get to their work — which left the night birds a couple of hours for a kip down.

But the new day promised better things. Rumour had it that there was a shop in Houndsditch which offered three dozen penny novelties at the knockdown price of eightpence. Eldorado reappeared on the horizon. There had to be another minor loan so that business could recommence, and a speedy start was made in Cheapside. But the best laid schemes ... By early evening total receipts amounted to eighteenpence. Somewhat disheartened our amateur salesman disposed of the balance of his stock to a fellow casual at a quarter of the purchase price, and determined that his last plunge would be on a barrel organ.

For this purpose he went into partnership with a friend and between them they raised the two shillings required for the hire of an instrument for the day. The organ bore a card which, in large letters, read: 'I am an Englishman' — a necessary announcement since many of the general public supposed that none but those of Italian race were organ grinders. Together they toured Gray's Inn Road, Guilford Street, Russell Square and Bedford Place and, later in the day, ventured into several back streets behind Piccadilly — all the while repeating their repertoire which ranged from excerpts from 'Il Trovatore' to 'Break the news to mother.' A profitable day ensured their survival over the weekend — thanks to the indispensable Salvation Army shelter.

What was learned from the week's experience? Principally that the casual's lot was a constant war with poverty and hunger. Few of them knew what a day might bring forth. A single man might get by, but no married man could support a wife and family on the uncertain takings of such chancy employment. The only options in such circumstances were for the wife and mother to go out to work; or with the children to undertake work at home; or for the husband to appeal for outdoor relief; or, having literally nothing left, to see his home break up as he entered the workhouse.

And if enquiry was made into the causes for his plight, the principal one was urban unemployment — that unwelcome word which, for long enough, C. S. Loch would place within inverted commas as if to dismiss it as some spectre of the Brocken. Personality weaknesses also played their part as did inadequate schooling — and the all pervasive evil of intoxicants could not be overlooked. With a sense of the realities of life, an early labour leader like Keir Hardie never failed to emphasise this. When secretary of the Ayrshire Miner's Union in the eighties, he counselled the miners to 'drink less . . . and think more.' At the founding of the Independent Labour Party at Bradford in January, 1893, he warned that 'the public house was the strongest ally of the usurer, the sweater and the landlord.' Nor was he alone in his judgment. In 1904, before a crowded Free Trade Hall in Manchester, John Burns declared in his florid style that 'the tavern has been the anteroom of the workhouse, the chapel of ease of the asylum, the recruiting station for the hospital, the rendezvous of the gambler, and the gathering ground for the jail.'

In his *Making of Victorian England*, Kitson Clark has confessed his bewilderment over the omission by many historians of the part which strong drink played in the miseries of Victorian England. It was a deciding factor in many a closely fought election where the candidate who could provide the largest number of electors with the greatest quantity of free beer usually won the day. Drunkenness was the cause of many a fracas between labourers, as those responsible for railway construction gangs knew to their cost. In extenuation it could be pleaded that life at the lower levels of Victorian society was made tolerable only by the anodyne of liquor. Fair comment — but its makers and purveyors could not escape their share of responsibility for the drug which made a man's last state worse than his first. In passing, it was no accident that the roughing-up of many a Salvationist in the eighties was encouraged by those whose profits depended upon the trade.

Meanwhile, *The Social Gazette* continued to pay as much attention to the economic as the personal reason for the widespread national destitution—one example of which was the plight of the women chain makers in the Black Country.

The illustrated front page for the issue dated July 7th, 1900, was taken up by a special correspondent's report on conditions and wages in the Cradley Heath area. Over a decade there had been a minimal improvement in the wage rate. In 1888 the Board of Trade's report to the government of the day quoted the price for the best half-inch chain as 2s. 9d. per cwt., which meant that a man, working a minimum sixty hour week, could earn from 8s. to 12s., and a woman from 3s. 6d. to 5s. 6d. By the spring of 1896 the price had risen to between 3s. 6d. and 4s. per cwt. and, by the turn of the century, to 5s. 6d. This meant that a man could earn 25s. to 30s. per week, and a woman 7s. to 12s.

Most of the two thousand men so employed worked in factories; most of the thousand to twelve hundred women in a large shed or shanty at the back of their home, and it was here that the most damaging effects of this heavy labour was to be seen. The long iron rod had to be heated to a white glow. In the factory this was done mechanically; in the outhouse behind the back door by hand operated bellows. The malleable rod was then bent, cut to the required length, and inserted into the last link of the existing chain. This new link was then closed by means of a heavy hand hammer and also by a spring tilt hammer operated by a wooden treadle fixed to the floor.

To work continuously in this overheated atmosphere took heavy toll of a woman's strength as well as her looks, and meant that her children — particularly those of pre-school age — could not be given the necessary care. It was argued by some that chain making was less unsuitable for a woman than work in a brickyard or galvanising factory. But those who knew — that is, those thus engaged six days a week — described it as 'no work for a woman.' Certainly not for the wages paid, for earlier wage rises were lost when the women's union ceased to function and under-cutting brought prices down. But on March 18th, 1907, as a result of negotiations between employers and employed, a rise of between ten and twenty per cent was agreed. Then on January 1st, 1910, the Trade Boards Act came into operation, providing a minimum wage rate for four selected industries — the cheaper forms of tailoring, cardboard box makers, the finishers of machine made lace — and the chain makers.

This fixed the new rate for a woman chain maker at 2½d. an hour, and a man from 5d. to 7½d. an hour. This was little enough in all conscience, but many a woman now doubled what she had been earning. Happily the Act had teeth, and *The Social Gazette* for September 9th, 1911, reported that one employer who, through ignorance or design, had paid less than the minimum, was brought to court and fined £30.

This now forgotten weekly never ceased to plead the cause of those who could not plead for themselves. One week there would be an article about the women who worked as walnut peelers and who were paid at the rate of 1s. 6d. per basket of a thousand walnuts. The expert among them could fill three baskets a day, and some even manage four. Thirty-six shillings for a week's work was wealth untold. Unfortunately the season only lasted six weeks but, for that brief interval, the walnut peeler was far better off than her sister in an East End factory where the weekly wage was rarely more but often less — than twelve shillings for a day which lasted from seven o'clock in the morning to six in the evening, with half-an-hour for breakfast, an hour for dinner and ten minutes for tea.

Three weeks later the *Gazette* gave a front page spread to conditions in some of the West End dressmaking establishments, quoting among other authoritative details, a report by a witness before the Royal Commission of Labour on the employment of women.

> Bond Street ladies' tailor. Refused to see me when I called to verify statements. Hours of labour: ordinary days, 8.30 a.m. to 8 p.m.; hours on Saturday, 8 a.m. to 4 p.m. Ten minutes for lunch. Time for dinner, half-an-hour. Time for tea, eaten while at work. Weekly wages: engaged at eighteen shillings, lowered to fifteen. Overtime: often till six on Saturday — no pay unless asked for ... Sanitary conditions bad. Gas stove in the room, no escape for fumes. No dining room or place to wash in.

Nor were isolated cases of distress ignored. The leader in the issue dated April 20th, 1907, was based upon a recent inquest on a child whose mother, deserted by her husband, supported herself by washing and cleaning but rarely earned more than 7s. a week. The grandmother contributed to the family income as much as she was able, but she worked at home trouser finishing for an English firm of tailors at 2d. per pair. The leader concluded by quoting some sentences of William Booth's from *In Darkest England*:

> These enormities, callously inflicted, are silently borne by their miserable victims ... Those firms which reduce

sweating to a fine art, who systematically and deliberately defraud the workman of his pay, who grind the faces
of the poor, who rob the widow and orphan and who, for
a pretence, make great professions of public spirit and
philanthropy, these men nowadays are sometimes sent to
Parliament to make laws for the people. The old prophets
sent them to hell . . .

9

Greedy of Gain

If William Booth had been beset by foes without, he was also assailed by fightings within — one result of which was the undesired resignation of Commissioner Frank Smith, his first choice for the leadership of the newly developing social service work for men.

Frank Smith became an officer in 1881 and, in the Army's turbulent days, was arrested for leading a march through the streets of London. Three years later William Booth showed his trust in this man of thirty by sending him to rally the Army in North America after the defection of Thomas E. Moore. On returning to England, and after a break in service in which ill-health played a contributory part, he was given oversight of the Social Reform Wing. *In Darkest England* was not published until October, 1890, but on Monday, December 29th, of that year, *The Times* carried a leader on the reason why he had resigned.

As might have been expected, William Booth was made the whipping boy. Mr. Frank Smith had been 'virtually cashiered.' An officer who had 'successfully managed the Whitechapel food and shelter depot' had been told to go by one who 'cannot have had an experience of business of this kind.' (Shades of the People's Market in 1870!) This was 'an unsatisfactory beginning' to the *Darkest England* scheme. 'I am no farmer,' William Booth was quoted as saying, and the leader went on to ask why then should he 'acquire an estate in Essex at £15 an acre' — this was land for the proposed farm colony at Hadleigh — and, for good measure, quoted the Melbourne *Argus* on the unsuitability of 'General' (in quotes) Booth settling 'reformed criminals and assisted paupers' in Gippsland and the Riverina.

In due course the froth died down — and perhaps one genuine clue to Frank Smith's action is found in his own biographer's observation that he 'found it impossible to confine himself solely to the interests of the Army.' Another clue may lie in the three questions which he addressed to William Booth concerning the administrative structure of this new development. Was there to be a distinct department responsible for implementing the social scheme? Was that department to be the social wing? Was he to be responsible for that department?

One question which does not seem to have been asked was: responsible to whom? This could have been the reason for the temperate comment of *The War Cry* on January 3rd, 1891, that 'this new section of our operations' must be 'fashioned according to the judgment of the General.' Fair enough! The money for this new venture had been raised on the faith of the general public in the integrity of William Booth. He could delegate authority but he could not abdicate responsibility. So Frank Smith found an opening on the recently formed London County Council, and Elijah Cadman followed him as Commissioner for the Social Reform Wing — a post he held for nearly ten years.

Meantime the work of implementing the *Darkest England* scheme continued. At least one of the institutions involved was established before William Booth began putting his thoughts on paper. The food and shelter centre in the West India Dock Road went back to 1888 (see page 38). The first elevator at 159, Hanbury Street — on the opposite side of the road to the first women's refuge (see p. 46) — opened its doors on June 29th, 1890, and by the time *In Darkest England* was off the press forty men were already working there.

The 'Elevator' was a new concept in social services, combining generous acceptance with patient but unwearying discipline. 'No one brings a reference here,' explained an officer in charge of one such institution. 'If a man is willing to work, he stays; if not, he goes.' No guide line could be simpler for the entrant; none more demanding upon those who were seeking his rehabilitation.

From the start William Booth made it plain that he would not have 'his customers pauperised.' 'There is no pretence of charity,' he added, 'beyond the charity which gives a man remunerative labour . . . What we propose to do is to enable those who are destitute to earn their rations and do enough work to earn their lodging until they are able to go out into the world and earn wages for themselves.' The elevator was, in effect, an early form of 'sheltered workshop' — a concept which was little known at the time and consequently less understood.

This was one reason for many of the charges of sweated labour, against which William Booth had always set his face. He appreciated the understandable sensitivity of the trades unions to this evil. He shared their feelings. He had given his word, when testifying before the Onslow Committee, that he would never use cheap labour to undersell the established market. In any attempt to improve the conditions of labour — as at the Lamprell Street match factory (see p. 110) — the wages paid were invariably higher than the accepted rate.

When, for example, in the summer of 1895 a charge was made that The Salvation Army was underpaying its printing employees, the works manager submitted the wage sheets for every man to the Printers' Labourer's Union, and invited the union secretary to go into the machine room and question whom he would. He found the rate above the trade union figure. No matter! Not even facts could stem the persistent and well publicised trickle of allegations that the men who voluntarily came into an elevator were overworked, underpaid and, as a final embroidery to the story, underfed.

Hanbury Street was the principle target of a self-appointed committee who staged a demonstration in Trafalgar Square. 'We have suffered too much in the past from

Christian philanthropy,' declaimed one orator. 'As soon as
the trading part of the Army is broken up, the religious part
will soon follow.' Another speaker demanded that every
man who entered Hanbury Street should be paid full trade
union rates. This was on a par with the question addressed
by an ill-advised Member of Parliament to the Home Secretary asking whether the Army's administration at Hanbury
Street did not contravene the provisions of the Truck Act.
Reason was powerless against such irrationality, so the
Parliamentary Committee of the Trades Union Congress
was persuaded to make its own investigation into conditions
at the elevator. Their subsequent report cleared the Army
on all counts.

But no sooner were these kinds of charges refuted than
they were resurrected. Within twelve months a London
newspaper repeated the accusation of sweating and under-
cutting, not forgetting the further charge of underfeeding.
The unfortunate inmates at Hanbury Street were being half-
starved. The answer to this charge was to publish the current
menu of three meals a day, seven days a week, and to point
to the visible physical improvement in the men who, arriving
at Hanbury Street weak and worn, were seen to be mending
after a fortnight or more of regular work, regular meals and
regular sleep.

As for underselling, Hanbury Street could not afford it.
'Cheap' labour was never cheap. Most unskilled men were
unable to produce a first class job at an economic price.
This was not their fault but their misfortune. Their uncertain
life had never allowed them to become skilled craftsmen.
What Hanbury Street did was to help those who were willing
to be helped to learn a trade which would in due course
entitle them to the rate for the job. Meanwhile the elevator
lost money — as the certified published accounts testified —
on this process of retraining hand and heart, but of this the
Army did not complain. Money spent in setting a man on his
feet was money well spent.

It was now left to the economic doctrinaires to keep the

fires of misrepresentation burning by charging William
Booth with usurping the function of the state. This must
have appealed to his gruff sense of humour, for it was
notorious that at this particular point in time neither of the
two principal political parties wished to become involved in
any form of industrial wrangle. They felt they were doing
enough if they kept the ring. So William replied that he
would be delighted to withdraw the moment the state was
willing to assume responsibility for the men who made Hanbury Street — or any similar institution — their sure port
in the economic storms of life.

But a minority would not let well alone and a blistering
resolution was placed on the agenda of the Trades Union
Congress at Nottingham in 1908. Against the advice of more
responsible delegates there were speeches which, for example, berated The Salvation Army as 'the most gigantic
fraud ever carried out under the name of religion.' But a
letter from William Booth placed before the Congress
revealed that he had already met a Trades Union deputation,
and he repeated in writing his observations on the points
discussed with them. (Present day readers will be aware that
our current forms of social security were then unknown and,
by many, undesired.) If Hanbury Street were to be closed,
he asked, what should he do with the men working there?
Should they be turned over to the unions? But they had no
cards and their membership was in default — if ever some
of them had belonged to a union. Should they be set adrift
on the open market where better men than they were unable
to find work? Or should he allow them to sink back into the
hopeless conditions which were theirs when first they sought
the help of Hanbury Street? 'These alternatives,' he concluded, 'I cannot face. I propose to go on helping these poor
fellows as far as I possibly can, and to place them in suitable
situations as soon as they are fit to take them . . . either in
this country or in some other.'

The resolution was withdrawn, and the only opposition
that remained was basically — and virulently — anti-

religious. An example of this change of temper was to be seen in the right-about-face of members of the Waltham-stow Labour League who heard 'with indignation' of the conditions prevailing at Hanbury Street, and forwarded to Elijah Cadman a strong resolution that labour be given 'her just dues.' An explanatory letter was sent to the secretary of the branch which he acknowledged in due course by enclosing copy of a further resolution. 'The sweating charges against The Salvation Army have been once more discussed and, in view of further information which has reached us, we have come to the conclusion that we are not in a position to express an opinion on this matter.'

The sitting member for Burnley, Mr. Fred Maddison, who had previously represented Sheffield (Brightside) in the Labour interest, commented that 'the Army is always liable to attacks of this sort, but in this instance they were over-done ... I am convinced that Salvationists are inspired by none but the loftiest motives and not by thoughts of personal profit.' Ramsay Macdonald, at the time secretary of the Labour Party, said that 'many of the men who sought the Army's help were in great need and desperately hungry, and it would be foolish to go into high and dry economics about work of that sort.' Perhaps the last word on this controversy was said by *Punch* — which in times past had not been guilt-less of satirical comment at the expense of William Booth — but now featured a cartoon which showed him leaving the annual Trades Union Congress in company with the President of the Local Government Board over the caption: 'Without a stain on their character.'

The efforts which William Booth was prepared to make to improve wages and conditions of labour had already been demonstrated in his opening of the Lamprell Street match factory on Monday, May 11th, 1891.

The plight of the unskilled female match workers was brought to the attention of the public by the successful strike led by Annie Besant in July, 1888. William Booth made his own enquiries into their need and, encouraged by his ex-

periment in setting up a mini-bookbinding factory to provide
employment for young women taken into the Army's rescue
homes in London (see *In Darkest England*, pp. 262ff.), resolved to establish a match factory where hygienic conditions and better wages would be the order of the day. So a
large building was bought in Old Ford, re-equipped for the
match-making business at a cost of £2,000, and a works
manager appointed who himself had suffered from phos-
phonecrosis or 'phossy jaw.' This usually began with severe
toothache, followed by a loss of one or more teeth. The
surrounding area of the jaw would then become infected —
which meant extensive surgery for the removal of the dis-
eased bone. The accompanying pain was intense, and for
some sufferers the end result was death.

In his privately produced booklet *The Darkest England
Match Industry* — from which, by permission of the author,
a number of facts have been taken — Mr. David C. Mitchell
quotes an H.M.S.O. report, printed in 1899, which gave the
number of deaths in England and Wales from phossy jaw
between 1882 and 1892 as fifty-five, with a further thirty-
seven between 1893 and 1899. The most dangerous place in
any factory was the workroom where the phosphorous paste
was made, though every worker was liable to infection.
Washing facilities were often inadequate, though there were
some girls who would not use the washrooms even when
these were provided. The reason why William Booth could
announce that no worker's health was in danger at Lamprell
Street was because the toxic yellow phosphorus was
nowhere used.

Wages were also raised. The average 2¼d. to 2½d. per
gross paid to employees in the industry was raised to 4d.
Thus the expert worker, turning out forty-five gross match
boxes per week would earn 15s. as against 9s. 4½d. The less
skilful, turning out twenty-five gross weekly, would be paid
8s. 4d. as against 5s. 2½d. The slowest worker whose output
was limited to twenty gross weekly would receive 6s. 8d. as
against 4s. 2d. elsewhere. Hours would be from 8 a.m. to

6 p.m., with an hour for the midday meal and two tea breaks at 11 a.m. and 4 p.m. respectively. The factory rule was to be 'Fair wages for fair work' — and this slogan appeared upon two of the earliest varieties of match boxes. Other labels read: 'Love thy neighbour as thyself'; 'Bear one another's burdens'; and 'Our work is for God and humanity.' These are now collectors' pieces.

Production presented few difficulties; those were associated with distribution and sales. The match industry in the United Kingdom employed some 4,300 people at this time. Lamprell Street had never more than 120 on its books. How was one small newcomer to elbow its way into a market where sales were divided between the non-safety phosphorus variety — responsible for phossy jaw — and the imported Swedish safety match which netted approximately £300,000 annually.

Sales promotion was transferred from the factory to the Army's Trade Department at Clerkenwell. A list of shops and agencies where *Darkest England* matches could be bought appeared in *The Social Gazette*, beginning with Aberdeen, Abersychan, Aberystwyth, Abingdon, Accrington, Aldrington, Alton, Altrincham, Ambleside, Amersham, Andover — and so on through the alphabet. At one time there were more than two hundred shops in the city of Leicester where these matches could be bought.

A British Match Consumers' League was formed with a card of membership, which read:

> I hereby pledge myself to buy and
> use only those matches which to the
> best of my knowledge and belief are
> (i) of British manufacture; (ii) made
> entirely free from sweated conditions;
> and (iii) free from any risk to the
> health and life of the worker.

An important N.B. in heavy type across the foot of the

card read: 'Members of the B.M.C.L. should "worry" their grocer, or other shopkeeper, who does not at present stock and sell these matches, at least twice a week until such time as he shall do so.'

Support for *Darkest England* matches came from across the board. When Mr. W. E. Gladstone was Prime Minister they were used at 10, Downing Street. The Bradford Board of Guardians instructed their contractor for groceries to supply safety matches as made by The Salvation Army. The President of the Chatham Trades Council successfully proposed a resolution that members should not purchase or use matches which required yellow phosphorus for their manufacture. This was sent to the Home Office as well as to the sitting member for Chatham, Viscount Cranborne, and copies were also hung in the local co-operative stores where members were urged only to buy matches made by The Salvation Army, as these were produced under the best conditions.

The War Cry for July 2nd, 1898, announced that Canon Wilberforce had persuaded one of the large departmental stores in London to stock *in Darkest England* matches, whereupon he preached a sermon in Westminster Abbey recommending his listeners to buy them. With fraternal greetings the Clapham branch of the Independent Labour Party urged members of the Central Finsbury branch to use Salvation Army matches — and none other.

From her home in Staffordshire the Duchess of Sutherland let it be known that 'the earnest ladies of the district are banding themselves together to bring the *Darkest England* matches into common use. I am giving them a fair trial at Trentham, and am very satisfied with them up to now.'

Despite all this enterprise, however, there was a sense in which the match factory failed, for it was taken over by the British Match Company on November 26th, 1901. But William Booth had never sought big dividends. What he had done was to accomplish his threefold objective and (1) make an effective protest against sweating; (2) raise the wages paid to the workers and (3) demonstrate that in the match industry human lives need not be placed at risk.

Even in 1895 Lamprell Street was still the one factory in the United Kingdom where only non-poisonous phosphorus was used, but increasing attention was being paid to the health of match factory employees. In August, 1897, the Act which prohibited the employment of young persons in dangerous occupations was extended to match making. In the following year the large factories in the country instituted regular dental inspection for their workers, paying sick benefit to employees suspected of having contracted phossy jaw. Some firms provided artificial teeth, where needed, without charge.

In the same year two French chemists discovered a satisfactory substitute for the dangerous yellow phosphorus, and patent rights were immediately taken out in Britain. In 1899 the government's Chief Inspector for Factories reported only three cases of infection, and a further three in the following year — all of which responded to treatment. By this time all the leading manufacturers were producing matches under safe conditions, though legislation totally banning the use of yellow phosphorus did not come into operation in Britain until the end of 1910 — nine years after the Netherlands had passed a similar law, nineteen years after Switzerland and twenty-one years after Sweden.

Lamprell Street was not a big business success story but, what was more important, William Booth was able to provide another demonstration of the truth that the social consequences of industry could not be ignored.

10

By Evil Report and Good Report

While Lamprell Street was slowly but surely demonstrating
that 'phossy jaw' was an unnecessary and avoidable hazard
in match making, William Booth was methodically developing part one of his *Darkest England* scheme which he called
'the city colony.' Within large and overcrowded urban areas
he proposed to set up a catchment basin where shelter, food
and temporary work could be provided for those who lacked
these basic necessities. This was no exercise in pious sentimentality, though it was inspired by love to God and man.
It was an open secret that he did not believe in, nor did he
propose to use the money entrusted to him, in what was then
called 'indiscriminate charity', though it is more probable
that those of his critics who most frequently mouthed the
phrase were least addicted to the practice. A leader in *The
Social Gazette* declared: 'A man has a right to demand that
his country shall supply him with work or food; the General's proposal is that he shall be supplied with both.'

In this matter William Booth was not a pioneer. London
had seen soup kitchens in operation in the eighteenth
century. In 1797 Patrick Colquhoun set up a committee
which fed some ten thousand people twice a week at a cost
of not more than one penny per meal. During the Napoleonic wars there were twenty-two centres in the capital from
which soup was distributed. In the winter following the
Peterloo Massacre the 'Committee for the Nightly Shelter
of the Houseless Poor' secured premises at London Wall and
were soon caring for two hundred inmates each night. At
first this was solely a winter activity but, when the cold was

severe and prolonged — as at the beginning of the reign of William IV — three shelters were opened providing for more than six thousand people. There were also night refuges — known as strawyards — in Victorian times. Possibly the oldest and largest in London was in Cripplegate, but later moved to Banner Lane, where the dormitories were heated by an outsize communal fire.

Yet even the worth of these was questioned. To have a place in which to sleep at night would encourage the idle and profligate to haunt the public house by day! Beside, were there not workhouses and casual wards for the homeless and starving? There were — but the principle of deterrence ruled with an iron rod in the kingdom of poor law relief. It was this fact which caused 'the labouring part of the community to regard the "parish" as the hardest taskmaster ... and the most unkind friend to whom they could apply.' The workhouse was deliberately made 'wholesomely repulsive.' But even before knocking at its forbidding doors there was a veritable *via dolorosa* to be trodden. The law of England was that no one could come upon the rates while he had anything whatever left to call his own. Not until an applicant possessed nothing other than the clothes in which he stood would he be admitted.

For the man who had not been driven so hard and was seeking only temporary relief, there was the casual ward or the 'spike.' Once again the principle seemed to be to make it as disagreeable as possible to the recipient. The medicine was to be made thoroughly unpleasant.

All this was common knowledge. In the nineties the editor of the *British Medical Journal* visited a workhouse where the sick

lay on plank beds with chaff mattresses about three inches thick between their weary bodies and the hard uneven planks ... Some idiots and imbeciles shared the wards with these patients. The infants occupied a dark stone paved room, bare of furniture, with no rug for the babies to crawl or lie upon, and no responsible person to see to their feeding or cleanliness.

In his *Portrait of an Age*, G. M. Young has written of 'the brutality that went on in some workhouses, the gorging in others, the petty tyranny of some officials and the petty corruption of Guardians.' This was not limited to scandal on an horrific scale as at Andover in the mid-nineteenth century but lasted on into the twentieth. *The Social Gazette* for May 17th, 1902, reported how an inmate declared in court that he had been assaulted, his eyesight impaired, and an attempt made to lock him in a cell by the assistant superintendent of the Paddington casual ward. At the hearing the magistrate found that the complainant had been assaulted and deprived of his liberty without cause or enquiry, and the defendant was fined forty shillings. Bramwell Booth was not exaggerating when, later, in his introduction to *The Salvation Army and Poor Law Reform*, he declared that 'no impartial person ... can wonder at the bitter, deepseated and unmitigated hatred with which a large proportion of people regard the whole poor law system, supposed to be designed for their benefit.'

To make doubly sure that facts supported his feelings, William Booth sent one of his officers, disguised as a loafer, to apply for admission to a London casual ward. The following sentences are taken from his report.

I stood outside the gate, answered a few questions, and then took the evening meal provided for me — a basin of 'stickfast' (note: thin gruel made with water but without sugar or salt) and a roll of dark bread ... I was then instructed to strip and enter the bath. There was no lack of ventilation; the big window just over the bath was wide open, as was the door. I plunged into the soup coloured water — plainly I was not the first to do so — and then searched for a spot on the towel which was not thoroughly wet ... Clad in the garb of Adam in the Garden, I then proceeded to the dormitory, found my bed and a short, white jacket — similar to a carpenter's or a glazier's — which was to be my night shirt. I donned it, wrapped two brown blankets around my damp person, gradually dried off, and tried to sleep in the open room with thirty other men . . .

At six o'clock we were wakened for breakfast — more 'stickfast' and bread — and from then until one o'clock picked oakum, of which four pounds had been given to each man . . . At dinner we were served with a piece of bread and a portion of salt Dutch cheese, and at six o'clock there was a final meal of 'stickfast' and dark bread . . .

By two o'clock an assortment of sores decorated my hands so that continued picking became painful in the extreme . . . but at which I laboured for twelve and a half hours consecutively, save for the single midday break. I was fortunate not to have been set the alternative task of breaking two or three cwt. of stones — a task as heavy, if not heavier, than that asked of many criminals in gaol . . .

As has already been noted, it was against such a grim background that William Booth opened his first cheap food and night shelter on February 18th, 1888, in the West India Dock Road, Limehouse — more than two years before *In Darkest England* was published. Additional shelters for men were opened shortly afterwards in St. John's Square, Clerkenwell, at 53 Lisson Street, at 272 Whitechapel Road, as well as in Horseferry Road, Westminster. Rough and ready these may have been, even crude to modern taste, but at least the treatment was humane. No one was assaulted either physically or verbally. Fervent prayer might make some men uncomfortable but it was preferable to endless cursing. What the needy thought about the Army shelters could be seen by the way they crowded them to the doors. Further accommodation was quickly provided — and fully occupied — in Blackfriars, Royal Mint Street and Charles Street, with provincial openings in Bristol, Bradford and Leeds. A labour bureau was attached to each of these three regional centres as well.

Thus by Christmas, 1894, just over four years after *In Darkest England* had come off the press, there were 3,500 beds available for men at a charge of twopence per night, and five hundred priced at one penny. There was also cubicle accommodation for another hundred men at three-pence per night, with two further shelters offering more than thirteen hundred men feeding, sleeping, reading and smoke room facilities from fourpence to sixpence per night. Hot and cold water, with towels, were available for all. In addition, there were two 'metropoles,' or working men's homes, in Southwark Road and Stanhope Street, known as 'The Ark' and 'The Harbour' respectively, where a private cubicle cost sixpence per night, and to these were later added 'The Lighthouse' in Quaker Street and 'The Anchor' in Bethnal Green.

Any man who was literally penniless could earn his over-night stay in one of the cheaper shelters by chopping fire-wood, but anyone in search of more regular employment could enter one of the four elevators — or 'sheltered work-shops' — in Hanbury Street, Montague Street, Maltby Street or West India Dock Road, or be taken on at the Salvage Wharf at Battersea. This last could employ up to three hundred men, most of whom stayed between two and three months. This meant that in any one year upwards of a thousand men benefited from this one institution — many of them going on to other employment when not transferred at their own request to the land colony at Hadleigh.

Yet, as volume three of the official history of The Salvation Army mildly observes, this good work was 'not at first welcomed by the local authorities.' There was, for example, the initial demand that a register should be signed by all who stayed overnight in an Army institution. Remembering that adult illiteracy was still widespread, this was officialdom in a wooden-headed mood. However, if signatures were wanted, signatures could be provided, and so it was not surprising that the highest and the lowest in the land, from the Heir Apparent to Jack the Ripper, stayed at one time or another under the Army's hospitable roof.

Next came the charge that the shelters were hotbeds of disease and the breeding ground of epidemics. In the summer of 1895 there was a smallpox scare and the condition of a man who had been admitted to Blackfriars was noticed by the officer in charge, who had him isolated immediately. Three calls were needed before a relieving officer arrived at midnight to confirm the infection and to order an ambulance — which did not reach the shelter, however, until four o'clock in the morning. In the event, it was discovered that the sick man had been turned into the street through the closing of a common lodging house in the district for which Dr. Joseph Waldo was responsible. Dr. Waldo was also responsible for Blackfriars, for he was the Officer of Public Health for the Vestry of Southwark. But Blackfriars — and Blackfriars alone — was placarded in the press as the culprit.

There was also the old lady who was taken into the women's shelter in Hanbury Street and whose decease was reported under such headlines as 'Old woman dies in unheated shelter.' At the resumed inquest the women who slept next to the deceased declared that the place was warm enough but that the old lady used to live on the bits of bread and tea given her. A juror elicited the fact that she had been admitted to the shelter without any money, and the doctor in attendance attributed death to syncope and debility brought on by previous exposure. The coroner gave his opinion that the shelter arrangements were admirable and a verdict of 'natural death' was returned. But the final verdict was not given the same publicity as the first scare headline.

In fact the campaign against the shelters increased rather than diminished. Standing logic on its head, *The Daily Chronicle* denounced them not because they were not clean but because some of their guests were dirty. A question was solemnly raised in the House, and inevitably a charge was laid that the Blackfriars shelter was overcrowded. The same Dr. Waldo inspected the building on behalf of the vigilant Vestry of Southwark and demanded thirty-six feet of ground space and three hundred cubic feet of air space for each inmate. William Booth was duly required to abate the nuisance for which his agents were responsible.

The unfortunate Southwark magistrate found himself involved in a Gilbertian battle between medical giants. The Salvation Army cannot be blamed for summoning its supporters in battle array — at their head Professor J. A. Wanklyn, sometime public analyst, Lecturer in Chemistry and Physics at the St. George's Hospital, national expert on air and water analysis, who declared on oath that he had taken samples of air at 11.40 p.m. in (1) the overflow room, (2) the large shelter and (3) the lower bunk room at Blackfriars and had found them entirely satisfactory. In his medical wisdom the Officer of Public Health required three hundred cubic feet of air space per man but this, commented *The Social Gazette*, was more than was given to many a first class passenger on an Atlantic liner, or to a member of Parliament at Westminster, or to most sailors in their bunks. Blackfriars already provided one hundred and eighty cubic feet per person. The *Gazette* hailed Professor Wanklyn as a Daniel come to judgment when he announced that he would be satisfied with one hundred and fifty, and rejoiced that Dr. Waldo had been 'pulverised.'

The *Gazette's* exultation was not shared by the harassed magistrate who delayed his judgment until it could be delayed no longer. Three months later he announced that, having visited Blackfriars himself, he had to agree that it was undeniably suited to the purpose for which it was being used. He could find no fault with the premises as such. 'On the question of overcrowding,' he continued, 'we have had the benefit of the advice of several medical authorities ... but they differ so widely ... that I think the wisest plan will be not to accept the evidence of either side in its entirety.'

With the impartiality of the law he then ruled that the capacity of the shelter should be reduced to 550 men, thus putting some 250 men on the streets although winter had already begun. The question which he did not consider, nor with which did the Vestry of Southwark concern itself, was where those 250 unfortunates were now to sleep.

This gave the press another field day, with *The Times* and *The Daily Chronicle* leading on. William Bramwell Booth answered *The Times*; George Scott Railton took on the *Chronicle*. Neither had a difficult case, and it was not hard for Bramwell Booth to rebut the charge that the Army's shelters were run as 'a commercial speculation' and that Blackfriars must make 'a handsome profit.' If they were so run, he rejoined, commercial prices would be charged — which one penny for a night's shelter was not, and the staff would be paid commercial salaries — which they were not. As for profits, the audited accounts for the year ended September 30th showed receipts of £2,954 and an expenditure of £2,648 — leaving a balance of £286, which did not even cover depreciation of furniture and fittings. The unkindest comment of *The Times* was that there was no reason 'for permitting him (i.e. Bramwell Booth) what was not permitted other people, viz. common lodging house keepers, who like himself made a profit out of a useful work.' This was decidedly unfair, but Bramwell Booth was content to describe the allegation as 'untrue.' 'Neither I, nor any other person, make any personal profit whatever out of the Army's social schemes.'

The police next tried their hand when they sought to have the long established women's shelter in Hanbury Street declared a common lodging house. This particular refuge was opened on March 10th, 1889, as a free shelter for women, with supper and breakfast supplied at threepence for an adult, twopence for children and at one penny for infants. Such a judgment would have been particularly damaging, not least because of the general reputation of such properties. 'It is scarcely possible,' said Shaftesbury in the House

of Lords, 'to describe the filthy condition of such houses —
the loathsome beds filled with vermin, the general overcrowding, the abandoned inmates, comprising the lowest
classes of vagrants, thieves and prostitutes.' Doubtless Hanbury Street had sheltered a few questionable characters.
That was why it existed. But it was neither filthy, nor vermin-
ous, not disorderly. Nevertheless William Booth was
charged in court with keeping an unregistered lodging
house, but the case was dismissed.

The police gave notice of appeal, but then changed their
tactics by bringing up instead a similar charge against another shelter altogether — the men's shelter at 272 Whitechapel Road. This time William Booth was found guilty,
but he in turn appealed, and Lord Justice Coleridge ruled
that a charitable institution, not carried on for profit or
personal gain, open only on such terms and to such persons
as the managers might direct, was not governed by those
Acts of Parliament which applied to places where 'all
persons were received for purposes of gain.' The conviction
was wrong and must therefore be set aside.

The Public Health committee of the London County
Council also tried to have 'The Harbour,' the Army's
metropole in Stanhope Street, licensed as a common lodging
house. This application failed as well, and the L.C.C. had to
bear the costs of the action. The committee was taken to
task at the next full meeting of the Council and, in addition,
had to endure a thorough castigation from Sir Walter
Besant in the pages of *The Daily News*.

There can be little doubt that these various attempts to
impose some kind of external constraint upon the Army's
social services were not made in the public interest, but
were an expression of a barely concealed prejudice against
The Salvation Army and all its works which continued to
exist in certain authoritarian minds. The true feelings of the
public can be judged from the relationship between the
Movement and the unemployed marchers of that day.

In the summer of 1905, 450 unemployed men tramped the

hundred miles from Leicester to London to plead their cause before the Prime Minister, Mr. Arthur Balfour. Mr. Ramsay Macdonald, then prospective parliamentary candidate for the city, asked the Army to feed the marchers while they were in the capital. (It may not be widely remembered that Mrs. Macdonald was the daughter of Prof. George Gladstone, for long associated with the Hove corps.) The building where the men were sleeping while in London was provided with blankets and bedding. Tea and supper on Friday, three meals on Saturday and Sunday, breakfast on Monday morning with a substantial packet of sandwiches to sustain the marchers on the first stage of their homeward journey, were supplied in a neighbouring shelter.

Of wider coverage still was the assistance given to a group of unemployed men who determined to march the 180 miles between Manchester and London in the late winter. They carried with them what was described as a 'Petition to the King.' Doubtless they would have settled with seeing the President of the Local Government Board for, as it transpired, they would not even have been received at several of their overnight stops but for the Army. The marchers had been warned in advance that they would have to take potluck with beds and meals, but at Hanley their leader made his way through the winter fog to the officer's quarters, only to find that he was leading a meeting in the Army hall. Meanwhile he himself had noticed some of the marchers hanging about the market place and had invited them into the warmth of his building. The upshot was that the whole company enjoyed Salvation Army hospitality overnight and the officer, who had slept with them, provided them with a hot breakfast in the morning.

The next day's tramp brought the men to Stafford where again no group was ready or willing to receive them — save the two single women officers who offered the shelter of the Army hall overnight. At Birmingham the men again fell back upon the Army, but at Coventry arrangements had been made for their reception. At Northampton, however, the Chief Constable appealed to the corps officer. The number of marchers had been swollen by those who had joined their ranks in Birmingham, but once again no local body — social or political — was prepared to welcome them. Supper was ready in the Army Hall, however, by the time they arrived, and a liberal covering of clean straw was spread over the floor of the young people's hall. 'The softest bed we've had for a week,' was the general comment. Then some of the Northampton bandsmen turned up with bandages and ointment for blistered feet and weary limbs. Not quite the oil and wine of the Good Samaritan, but as near as made no difference.

11

Mercy on the Poor

Even while the city colony was only in its early stages of development, William Booth took formal possession of the initial eight hundred acres of land which formed the basis of the proposed farm colony at Hadleigh — the second phase of his scheme of social reclamation.

The farm he had in mind had to be within reasonable distance of London, with good communications by rail and water, though sufficiently removed from large centres of population to be free of the temptations of urban life. The land should be freehold, suitable for market gardening, but with sufficient clay to provide for brick making, not forgetting adequate grazing ground as well. Perhaps no dream is ever fully realised, but the three thousand two hundred acres which were finally acquired fulfilled in due course many of the hopes entertained for the colony — though not without much toil and trouble, for the scheme was intended:

To provide work on the reclamation or improvement of land upon which unskilled labour could be profitably employed.

To make use of hand labour to the largest possible extent so as to afford useful training to those who wished to undertake farm work either at home or overseas.

To develop such industries as are immediately related to farming, and

To help the men working on the colony to develop their own powers — morally and mentally — and to prepare themselves for a worthy return to community life.

The colony itself was an amalgamation of three smaller farms containing a large area of rough pasture, about a tenth of which would have to be ploughed up. A section of eighty acres along the northern boundary of the colony was in first class condition, but to the south there lay a stretch of saltings which was periodically covered by high spring tides. One proposal was to wall these off with a dyke and then dress the soil so heavily that crops might be planted. Of more immediate advantage was the loading and unloading of cargoes from barges provided by this access to the river, and later on a tramway linked the Hadleigh brickfields to the wharf.

Accommodation had first of all to be built to house the colonists, and so on May 5th, 1891, Bramwell Booth wrote to his father — then conducting public meetings in Lausanne — proposing an expenditure of £1,500 on dormitories, dining room, kitchen, laundry and ablution blocks, equipped with beds, chairs, stoves, crockery and cooking utensils, to take 180 men — one hundred to work on the land, forty in the brickfields and forty on ancillary duties.

A group of thirty men — later increased to seventy-five — made up the first arrivals, chosen mainly because of their fitness to work on building sites. These were temporarily housed in the Castle Farm house and an adjacent barn dormitory. By the late autumn four of the five dormitories were ready for use, as were the kitchen, ablutions and laundry. What is of interest is that a sheaf of barley and some outsize vegetable marrows added to the current harvest festival display in the Hadleigh parish church.

The selection of trainees for Hadleigh would have taxed the judgment of a Solomon. To begin with, most were unskilled and unwanted on the open labour market. Some unfortunate who had slept for a couple of nights under a hedgerow would claim to be a practised farmhand, and a down-and-out who had once held a horse's head would declare that he had been 'used to horses' all his life. All the same, it was hard to lose patience with some poor devil who, as he was being interviewed for Hadleigh, caught a glimpse of a promised land flowing with milk and honey — or so he thought. Early on, a rule had to be made that applicants would first have to work for a month in an elevator, and thereafter serve on the colony for another month for food and maintenance — though this did not apply to any man who could give proof of specific agricultural skills.

By the autumn of 1894 — just over three years after the initial deposit had been paid — the farm, dairy, market garden, nursery, poultry and industrial sections were all in operation. Wheat, oats, barley and rye were being raised, together with roots for consumption and seed. The stock included five hundred head of cattle, two hundred of sheep and over five hundred pigs. The dairy contained some eighty cows and heifers and the total milk yield was being sold at prevailing prices. Seventy-five men were employed on over two hundred acres of fruit and market gardening. Seventy acres of fruit trees had been planted by the colonists themselves, and a small nursery had been established. Much of this success was due to the skill with which the various superintendents oversighted their untrained labour force. In the same year some three million bricks were produced by the brickfields, and a small steam joinery helped to meet the domestic necessities of the colony. A bakery on site also supplied the needed bread. By this time the completed dormitories could house 350 men, and a sick bay within the grounds was equipped to take sixteen patients. A hall seating five hundred people had also been erected for worship on Sunday and a variety of meetings on weekdays.

The record reads impressively — and such it was, especially when the human returns were studied. In the first three years just under fifteen hundred men passed through Hadleigh. Out of every hundred, thirty-nine left for work with satisfactory references; eighteen went to recommended situations; ten returned to friends or enlisted in the Armed Forces; ten left without notice on their own account;

twenty-three were discharged as unsatisfactory — mostly due to drunkenness and/or unwillingness to work.

But this encouraging result from an experiment for which there was no blueprint, was not secured — to take the least important factor — without continuous financial anxiety. William Booth had hoped that the colony — like his other remedial enterprises — would break even. That was all he asked. He was not out to make money but to remake men. The annual income of £30,000 for which he had asked was for improvements and contingencies. In the event, as he disclosed in his Queen's Hall speech, he was receiving little more than £3,000 annually.

The inevitable mishaps duly occurred. On November 14th, 1894, Bramwell had to report to his father that one of the Hadleigh barns had been burned down with a total loss of its contents. Three weeks later, with the accounts for the financial year before him, he had to report a loss on the colony's working of some £2,000. Examination showed that part of this was due to a sharp decline in the value of stock in hand. Hay which, during the drought of the previous year, had been worth £4 a ton, was now worth only half that figure. Though the number of horses on the farm had increased, their total book value was £500 down. However, the overall loss was levelling out. In 1892 it was £6,000; in 1893 £3,700; in 1894 £2,100. By 1897 the annual loss had fallen to £700 on a total turnover of £35,000. So toiling, rejoicing, sorrowing — but ever seeking to become more efficient — the Colony advanced from experiment to acceptance. Not surprisingly, there were its imitators.

In the summer of 1893 the Poplar Board of Guardians arranged a conference with Guardians in neighbouring areas in order to consider the possible purchase of land in Essex for the establishment of a farm colony, wages to be paid half in food, half in money, with imprisonment for those who were found to be enjoying the benefits of the colony without complying with its conditions. George Lansbury pronounced himself in favour of the proposal without committing himself to precise conditions. 'I contend,' he wrote, 'that London can, under the Acts of Elizabeth and William IV, now at once, through Boards of Guardians, take over land and start a colony in which farming could be carried on by the most improved methods of agriculture, and that such farming would provide all the necessities of life for those who did the work as well as their dependents.'

For this, however, he had to wait until 1904 when an American business man with an interest in social reform, Joseph Fels, purchased one hundred acres of land near Laindon and offered it to the Poplar Board of Guardians for three years at a peppercorn rent, with the option of buying the farm at the price which he had paid at the end of that period. Hitherto the Local Government Board had refused to sanction any such schemes out of public money, but now permission was given. Mr. Fels followed this up by an offer on similar terms of a 1,300 acre farm at Hollesley Bay in Suffolk which would provide work for between five and six hundred men.

In wishing well to both enterprises *The Social Gazette* rightly observed that much would depend upon the dedication of the staff. A good man could overcome the defects of an inadequate system, but a poor man would fail with the best possible system. Further, these new ventures lacked authority to pay the men by means of any kind of piece-work system, whereas at Hadleigh men were rewarded as they progressed. Another small but vital weakness at Hollesley was that there was no choice of food. In a paper read that year before an international congress in Edinburgh, Colonel David C. Lamb (who had been Governor at Hadleigh for five years) said that experience had taught him that an important step towards restoring a man's self-respect was to allow him a choice of what he might eat. The difference might be only between mashed swedes or boiled peas, rice pudding or plum duff, but it did wonders for morale. The *Gazette's* final point was that the rehabilitation work at Hadleigh was 'unashamedly based on faith in the power of

God to change a man's life' — a fact which Beatrice Webb noted when she visited the Army colony herself.

George Lansbury was not the only one to see Hadleigh as a pattern which could be followed. Various London Boards of Guardians had already decided that some of their own hard cases might profit from a term at Hadleigh, and Camberwell made its own approach. In the faith that there is nothing too hard for the Lord the colony authorities agreed, though it is hoped that they made the valid theological point that even the grace of God calls for human co-operation.

Over the year the Camberwell Guardians sent eighty-nine of their 'able-bodied paupers' to Hadleigh. All were volunteers; less than half of them were under thirty-five years of age; twelve of the rest were over fifty. Without doubt the majority were willing to work, but twenty-five of the group were found to be unfit for regular physical labour. Nevertheless, by the end of the year one-third of the men were still working at Hadleigh, and one-third had been placed elsewhere. Half of the rest had gone off on their own to find employment while the remainder did not want to work.

The Camberwell Guardians were realists enough to announce that 'the scheme, as far as it had gone, might be considered fairly satisfactory as a first experiment and ... with the consent of the Local Government Board, would be continued for a further period of six months.' The *Local Government Journal* declared that 'the results ... at Hadleigh are now sufficient to show that a start may safely be made in a new country. It is true that the percentage of paupers turned into honest, industrious men has not been high, but those who know the pauper class never expected it would be ... But if only ten per cent accomplish the task and satisfy the test, the scheme will have justified itself.' Other Boards of Guardians apparently agreed — for those of Mile End, Islington, Greenwich, Lewisham and Hackney began to negotiate with Hadleigh on similar terms. The arrangement generally included a weekly capitation grant of five shillings for each man received, while the Guardians continued to provide for his family at home.

The President of the Local Government Board seemed to be satisfied as well, for in the autumn of 1895 Mr. Henry Chaplin paid a further visit to the Colony. 'I am much indebted to the officers . . . for the courtesy with which they showed me all I desired to see and . . . wish them success in their good and admirable work.' Such an event was national news and in Edinburgh *The Scotsman* cautiously commended the Army for trying 'to teach a rather helpless class of the community something about farming and market gardening . . . The land was in rather a wretched condition when they took possession, and it is remarkable what they have done with the heavy clay soil covering the greater part of the estate . . . A number of men in a very destitute condition who were sent to the Farm Colony have turned out well, although a percentage were worthless loafers who have no wish to do an honest day's work at farming or anything else.'

The Bristol Mercury struck a more cheerful note: 'The only hopeful sign for really beneficial legislation that we can perceive is the visit of Mr. Chaplin to the flourishing farm colony for the unemployed in Essex. Of course, everyone knows that the relief of pauperism effected by this particular colony is but a drop in the bucket . . . but the very fact of Mr. Chaplin's visit proves, we hope, that the government is not only thinking seriously of relieving local taxation by making the relief of pauperism a national instead of a local burden, but that a stupendous effort is about to be made to cut out the cancer of vagrancy from our social system.'

'Flourishing' was the right word. By the turn of the century the colony had outlived its growing pains and was divided into nine sections, each under a skilled superintendent responsible to the Governor. The farm proper covered the grazing and arable lands; the market garden the fruit growing and the nurseries; the engineering the maintenance of all domestic machinery; the reception centre the

intake and initial training at Leigh Park; the works department the internal services; the stores the supplying of the
colonists' personal needs; the home and social covered
catering, sick bay, library, laundry and similar amenities;
the poultry and the brickfields were also separate entities.
Yet at this point in time the year's administrative overheads
— including the allowances paid to the Governor and staff,
plus postages and stationery, travelling and other in-
cidentals — amounted to £835.

For the last year of the century *The Times* analysed the
intake of 775 men. As all were free to come, all were free to
go — and 193 chose to do so, some after so brief a stay as to
deprive the colony staff of any real opportunity of helping
them. Forty-seven were discharged for drunkenness or unwillingness to work. Over three hundred satisfactorily
completed the training course and secured work or returned
to friends. In other words, two out of five made good, a
figure which is all the more remarkable when it is remembered that these men were admitted to Hadleigh not
because of their previous skills but on account of their past
failures. *The Times* concluded by saying:

> . . . In so condensed an account of the Colony's present
> state, scarcely a notion can be given of the great improve-
> ment wrought in the colonists themselves, without which
> no improvement in plant or property could make the
> experiment anything but a failure . . . The strengthening
> of moral fibre, the rebuilding of shattered character, and
> the restoration to physical health of the broken down are
> remarked by all who have the opportunity of observing
> the same colonists week by week.

The Treaty of Vereeniging which ended the Boer War in
1902 gave Britain an opportunity to devote her undivided
attention to her domestic needs — and not before time. The
eleventh annual report of the Board of Trade showed that
the average weekly wage was declining for at least nine out of

every ten workers in the country. The fall in 1901 was
1s. 9¼d. per man; in 1902 1s. 8d.; in 1903 a further eleven-
pence — making a total reduction of 4s. 4¼d. per man since
the beginning of the century. These sums appear trivial
today but this was a time when — to quote David Lloyd
George on his own hard-pressed boyhood — a sixpence was
'a coin of destiny.'

The number of the unemployed was rising. The figure for
1904 was higher than in any year since 1874. Evidences of
widespread physical deterioration were to be seen before
children were in their teens. There was a difference of as
much as five inches in the height of boys of 11/12 years of
age drawn from opposite ends of the social scale. A government committee was set up to examine the overall situation,
and a deputation who visited Hadleigh saw for themselves
what Lady Warwick discovered when, for five months in the
winter of 1903, some 70/80 men from the colony worked on
the gardens of her Essex home at Easton Lodge. *The Nineteenth Century* quoted her as saying:

> Their labour was not quite so rapid as that of the skilled
> working man who keeps his muscles in good training, but
> this was due to a lack of physique. Most of them, however,
> made up for this lack of strength by the willing and per-
> severing spirit which they showed. The Salvation Army
> had, in fact, achieved a remarkable result in a short time
> with a class that is generally considered most unpromising.

Forget the faint air of superiority. The nineteenth century
cannot be blamed for not sharing the 'all men are equal, only
some are more equal than others' notion of the twentieth.
The 'class' was not so 'unpromising' as Lady Warwick supposed. What was unpromising was the inability on the part
of their rulers to take any action to promote their welfare,
for all that Mr. Walter Long, as President of the Local
Government Board, could do was to place the responsibility for the unemployed in any particular area upon the

shoulders of an ad hoc group of town councillors, poor law guardians and social workers, financed by voluntary contributions. In the following year — 1905 — every borough with a population of 50,000 and over was required to set up a distress committee similar to that at work in London. Some overheads might be charged to the rates, but proposals for relief work were still to rely on voluntary support.

All this made a proven pilot scheme like the Hadleigh farm colony shine through the gloom of public uncertainty. Though at long last it was becoming increasingly clear that the cure for unemployment was beyond the scope of individual effort, here was a plan which could provide work and help restore a man's self-respect. On economic grounds alone it merited attention, even though the Charity Organisation Society maintained its traditional view that the real cause of unemployment was 'only partly industrial and economic. In great part it was a problem of social competence and moral responsibility.' But when in 1906 Westminster made an exchequer grant of £200,000 to replace Queen Alexandra's distress fund which had raised £150,000 in the previous year, and repeated the grant in 1907 and 1908, the state had taken the first step towards admitting that the provisions of the existing poor law were not enough.

Meanwhile the 1903/04 Mansion House Fund had been working closely with the existing farm colonies at Hadleigh and Osea Island. The published report indicates the swing in public opinion.

> The value of colony relief works, both as a test and as a method of relief, has been thoroughly established. The offer of continuous work deters the idle ... (and) also offers the minimum attraction to vagrants throughout the country likely to be drawn to London by rumours of unconditional relief. To those who are helped the relief provided is thorough, and at the same time they are prevented from unfairly competing in the labour market with their unassisted neighbours.

On Hadleigh in particular the report said:

> There was a most marked change in the physical con-
> dition of the men toward the end of their stay. The regular
> diet, fresh air and outdoor employment improved the
> health of all of them and made them into strong robust
> men. It was noticeable that they also improved in appear-
> ance ... In every sense of the word the men were better
> fitted to obtain and retain employment at the end of their
> stay than they were say, a month after their arrival.

Within days of this report appearing, William Booth was
offering to take on another four hundred married men at
Hadleigh on the same terms — providing them with board
and lodgings plus fifteen shillings per week as a contribution
to the needs of their homes during the retraining period.
Further, if the President of the Local Government Board
would furnish the necessary capital to provide temporary
accommodation and the required tools, he would take on
another six hundred, making a thousand in all. The proposal was welcomed on both sides of the House. Mr. Will
Crooks made the point that the only way in which a man
could make sure of obtaining food, shelter and work was to
break the law. Then prison took care of these basic needs.
A more excellent way was surely to train — or retrain —
him in more profitable skills, as at Hadleigh.

Sir John Gorst — a Liberal Unionist along with Joseph
Chamberlain — had already introduced into the Commons
a bill to amend the Vagrancy Act of 1824 by extending the
farm colony principle throughout the country, and an inter-
departmental committee was set up to study his proposals.
The committee met, deliberated and recommended — but
there was a general election in December, 1905. The new
ministry launched its own social measures, the most notable
of which was the introduction of non-contributory old age
pensions, and little more was heard of Sir John Gorst's
plans. But this did not affect the ongoing work at Hadleigh

which was independent of changes in the party political scene. One thing was plain — the better the work of the colony was understood, the more widely was it commended.

One of the final actions of the outgoing government had been to set up a Royal Commission on the Poor Law and the Relief of Distress from Unemployment, which issued a Majority and Minority Report in January, 1909. The chairman was Lord George Hamilton; among the members were half-a-dozen leading figures from the Charity Organisation Society, a sprinkling of Poor Law administrators, clergymen — and Beatrice Webb, possibly the most purposeful and resourceful of them all. Nothing less than first-hand information would do for her, so she visited both Hollesley and Hadleigh in quick succession. Her entries, quoted from *Our Partnership* (by kind permission of The London School of Economics and Political Science) read:

> January 13th, 1908. A weird Christmas recess at Hollesley Bay colony, investigating the daily routine of the three hundred men's lives ... The atmosphere — the impression of the place was mournfully tragic — half-educated, half-disciplined humans, who felt themselves to have been trampled on by their kind, were sore and angry, every man of them in favour of every kind of protection against machinery, protection against female, boy and foreign labour, protection against the Irish, Scotch and country men, protection against foreign commodities, protection against all or anything that had succeeded whilst they had failed ... A faint-hearted, nerveless set of men, their manner sometimes servile, sometimes sullen, never easy and independent.

On the following February 2nd she spent a weekend at Hadleigh 'watching The Salvation Army at work among the unemployed and the unemployable.' She wrote:

> The most interesting fact is The Salvation Army itself.

I have seen something of the officers in London: Colonel Lamb, Colonel Iliffe, Commander (sic) Cox and others, all belonging to the social side ... In respect to personal character, all these men and women constitute a *Samurai* caste, that is, they are men and women selected for their power of subordinating themselves to their cause, most assuredly a remarkable type of ecclesiastic: remarkable because there is no inequality between men and women, because home life and married life are combined with a complete dedication of the individual to spiritual service. A beautiful spirit of love and personal service, of content and joy, permeates their work; there is a persistent note of courtesy to others and open-mindedness to the world ...

How does Hadleigh differ from Hollesley? A more mixed lot of men — ex-convicts, ex-tramps, workhouse able-bodied picked up in shelters but, on the other hand, less of the ordinary ruck of casual labourers. Here they are, I think, more successful in getting the men to work; there is less foul talk; perhaps less discontent and jeering. The self-devotion of the officers counts for something in raising the tone of the colonists ...

The last line provides the clue to the difference between the various farm colonies — only in place of 'something' should be written 'much.' Mrs. Webb found what she called 'the religious pressure ... intensely compelling.' Compelling — maybe; coercive — no; but essential — yes.

Wisdom was justified of her children, for reports of indiscipline elsewhere began to circulate through the country. The press that had lampooned William Booth now cartooned George Lansbury and Will Crooks as enjoying themselves 'on the house', smoking Churchillian size cigars and calling for their glasses to be refilled, though both men were lifelong non-smokers and total abstainers. A government enquiry was set up and both leaders were vindicated, but they deserved more generous treatment for their pains.

Canon Barnett had formed his own shrewd judgment of

what made Hadleigh tick. 'We never found' (he wrote) 'that the Hadleigh people strained their authority in the matter of religion. Their treatment struck us as being thoroughly regenerative.' And regeneration of the individual and community, of the community and the individual, was the goal which William Booth ever had in mind.

12

Neither do I Condemn

Before dealing with what William Booth described as 'the third and final stage of the regenerative process — the colony over-sea,' some account must be given of what was undertaken under the *Darkest England* scheme on behalf of women and girls. This was inevitably spread against a more diversified backcloth than the institutional work for men, though the word 'institutional' must not obscure the truth that even the elevator — as William Booth called his sheltered workshops — was made for man, not man for the elevator. But the varied needs of women had to be seen in terms of a fireless grate, the deserted wife, the aged and ailing widow, the hungry child, the pregnant girl, the disillusioned street walker and the underpaid mother working to support a fatherless family.

As often as not the prostitute was as much the product of poverty as of total depravity, though the corrupting influence of male demand must not be overlooked. Of conditions in the Victorian countryside no less an authority than William Acton declared that 'the seduction of girls is a sport and habit with vast numbers of men, married and single, placed above the ranks of labour.' Nor was the situation any better in the towns. 'To keep female domestics virtuous for any length of time' (he continued) 'was ... often impossible.' The raising of the age of consent did not put an end either to seduction or promiscuity. In the climate of the times the scales were tilted heavily against the women. Justice was not merely painted blind; she indeed was blind. A putative father might suffer a weekly payment of eighteenpence if his bastard lived. If the child died, he was free of legal obligation.

It says much for William Booth's sense of balance that he devoted little more than a dozen pages of *In Darkest England* to what he called 'the career in which the maximum income is paid to the newest apprentice.' He never claimed to be the first in this, or any other, field of human need. So far as 'fallen' women were concerned, 'the Butlers preceded our own pioneering,' said a Salvationist tribute which was linked with the centenary celebrations for Mrs. Butler. What William Booth wanted was to drop the adjective. That — and kindred — terms, he declared in his personal introduction to the first volume of regulations for social officers, are 'repugnant to the whole purpose of our efforts as they are opposed to the words of Jesus . . . I hope the day may soon come when it will be possible to abandon them for ever.'

Doubtless it was their unrelenting awareness of the realities of life which endeared the followers of William Booth to Josephine Butler. Of some of the straiter sect of evangelicals she wrote: 'They don't want to know of them . . . (They) have numerous conferences for the deepening of spiritual life, from which they come away gorged with spiritual foodstuffs. What is the use of these conferences when they . . . leave the hell around as bad as before?' Not so the Salvationists. They did not wait upon the production of a book, even so seminal a volume as *In Darkest England and the Way Out* before taking action. 'It is the spontaneity of all outward expressions of the spiritual life which is their *raison d'être* . . . and gives them the grace they possess, in my eyes at least,' said Mrs. Butler.

It was this spontaneity which marked the efforts of Mrs. Cottrill, told in chapter four, as it marked the opening of a rescue home for women in Glasgow in the spring of 1883. This folded up within the year, but this temporary failure was offset by the renting of a small house in Hanbury Street (a thoroughfare still linking Commercial Street and Vallance Road in Whitechapel) in 1884. This mustard seed

of a beginning started with two girls. But within ten years
some fifteen hundred women were being received annually
in the fourteen homes which were divided equally between
London and the provinces.

Analysis showed that about half this number had been
living by prostitution; the other half came from backgrounds
which were equally unsatisfactory, either socially or economically. The publication of the 1894 social report also
showed that there were now two night shelters housing
upwards of four hundred women at a time, with three
metropoles offering accommodation at fourpence or sixpence per person. Three lodging houses had also been
opened for working women and, in addition to the maternity home at Ivy House, 271 Mare Street, Hackney, there
were three maternity posts in South Hackney, Clapton
Park and Limehouse Causeway respectively. A notice in
The Social Gazette announced that 'for 7s. 6d. there can be
obtained the services of a certified midwife and nurse. Will
attend mother and child for nine days before and after confinement. In need the fee is reduced or waived.' Alterna-
tively, the concluding sentence read: 'The fee can be paid in
weekly instalments.'

With unnecessary gracelessness the *Record* remarked that
'it would be interesting to know if The Salvation Army
required that its nurses should go through the hospital
ranks ... or whether new recruits, after a few months'
training, where allowed to don the uniform and pose as
guardians of the sick.' The proverbial soft answer invited
the writer to voice his concern to the officer in charge at Ivy
House, though without warning him that he ran the risk of
being sent away with the Scriptural equivalent — if there
is one — of a flea in his ear. For in charge at 271 was
Elizabeth Sapsworth, of independent mind and means, who
lived to see five hundred nurses trained at Ivy House, more
than two hundred and fifty pupils obtain the Central Midwives Board Certificate, and nearly eight thousand births
attended by Ivy House district nurses before the work was

transferred to the Mothers' Hospital in Lower Clapton
Road, opened by Princess Louise on October 18th, 1913.
The man from the *Record* could not have dreamed that from
the same stock as those nurses whose skills he affected to
despise would come the woman officer — Colonel Frances
Foxton — who was President of the Royal College of
Midwives from 1963 to 1965 inclusive.

Far from this work being undertaken by bumbling do-
gooders, William Booth had placed these manifold activities in the hands of Mrs. Bramwell Booth, wife of his eldest
son. Though still in her early twenties, with her first baby
often lying asleep in a clothes basket in her office, she
began to gather around her a group of women whose concern was matched by their competence. Chief among these
mature people was Adelaide Cox, of Anglican stock, who,
standing quietly in the Broad, Oxford, on the spot where
Ridley and Latimer were martyred, accepted Jesus as
Saviour and Lord while repeating the first verse of Charlotte
Elliott's 'Just as I am, without one plea.' She served with
Mrs. Booth for twenty-four years before succeeding her as
leader of the Women's Social Services.

Closely associated with her for thirty-seven years was
Elizabeth Lambert, whose skill as a counsellor was born of
her unaffected communion with Christ. After her death her
song book showed that she had heavily underscored the lines:

> Within my heart, O Lord, fulfil
> The purpose of Thy death and pain,
> That all may know Thou livest still
> In blood-washed hearts to rule and reign.

Another of the same spiritual family was Mary Bennett,
who forsook the comforts of her cultured circle for the
service of those who, in Kingsley's phrase, had 'lost their
way.' From exhibiting the work of hand and eye at the
Royal Academy, she turned to the more demanding task of
renewing the divine image in human lives.

Time would fail to tell of the twenty-five year old Mari-
anne Asdell, matron of the Army's first home in Great
Britain for young children; of the middle-aged Alice Barker
who found release from the sorrow of her own widowhood
in the service of her sex; of Mrs. Reynolds who, along with
Elizabeth Combe, saw that the teenage Eliza Armstrong
came to no harm during the Maiden Tribute storms of 1885;
of Mrs. Frost, a midwife from the Channel Islands, who
helped to staff the first midnight patrol post in the Charing
Cross area, and then to establish in Chelsea the maternity
centre which preceded Ivy House; or of Mrs. Sowdon —
possibly of even wider professional experience — who forsook the assured rewards of her comfortable clientele for the
frugal allowance of a single woman Captain serving, and
teaching others to serve, where the need was greatest.

For her part, the young Mrs. Booth was dismayed by
some of the refuges she visited in search of experience.
Rooms were bare and dismal. Bolts and bars were every-
where. The main occupation was laundry work. No one
over twenty-five years of age was admitted. No girl, whatever her age, was admitted with a baby. No girl who got into
trouble after a term in the refuge was given a second chance.
The whole atmosphere was penitential, whereas a girl at that
critical point in her life needed not condemnation but an
understanding welcome. 'They require support,' wrote Mrs.
Booth, 'in their final efforts to earn their living and then to
return to society.'

Realising that there was an economic as well as a moral
problem to be solved, home industries were commenced
— a book-binding factory in Rawsthorne Street, off Goswell
Road, a knitting factory in Upper Clapton, a laundry in
Stoke Newington. Domestic service of the 'Upstairs, down-
stairs' variety was the well-trodden path of the working girl
in Victorian times, so a register was compiled of mistresses
needing servants, and of servants seeking a post. The information sought was as searching in the one instance as
the other. Even domestic service required a 'character' or a

'reference', and almost as indispensable was the box of personal clothing required by any girl who thought of living-in. Systematic after-care supported the morale of the girl going out to her first place, and the cost of her basic outfit could be paid back, by mutual arrangement, on easy terms. All this helped to provide an alternative trade to the streets.

This union of common sense touched by divine grace was as much the reason for the success of a collective farm such as Hadleigh as of the personalised approach needed with every woman and girl. No idealist more down to earth than those who worked with William Booth, yet none more certain that 'except the Lord build the house, they labour in vain that build it.' How else could they face situations which made the most lurid Victorian melodrama read like a Sunday school prize?

Take this real life story drawn from the first decade of this work for women. A country girl of twenty-six was seduced by a farm hand who promptly deserted her when he found that she was pregnant. Rejected by her home, her only refuge was the workhouse where, until forbidden by law, the unmarried mother-to-be was required to wear a conspicuous yellow dress. When this was banned, some workhouse authorities substituted a dress with a single vertical yellow stripe. Misfortune was not to be hidden. Meanwhile the girl's mother died and, when her baby was born, she returned to her native village in the hope of finding shelter for the child while she went out to work for its support — but without success. Even her own relatives refused her and, in desperation, she took the child's life, was arrested, tried, found guilty of wilful murder, sentenced to death and spent eight days in the condemned cell before her punishment was commuted to penal servitude for life. After serving six years she was released by order of the Home Secretary and handed over to the Army's care — looking like a woman of fifty. Her father, who was present in court during her trial, lost his power of speech while listening to the sentence of death being passed, and never said another word.

Not all the 1,414 women and girls in Britain who sought the Army's help in that particular year (1894) had so horrific a story, but it may be said with confidence that there was not one for whom prayer was not offered, or who was not reminded of the gospel which is the power of God unto salvation. Perhaps that is why though just over twenty per cent failed to respond to help and were discharged as unsatisfactory, just over half the total number were found work, while over a quarter returned to friends, were married, or emigrated. After three years a further follow-up of a hundred girls gave fifteen as having relapsed, but forty-two still in a situation with forty-three who had married, were with relatives or friends, or were otherwise happily provided for.

At no time did the needs of women and girls who sought the Army's help spring from a single cause. Character weaknesses and unavoidable poverty were sometimes interwoven past all unravelling. For example, the young could be at the mercy of an employer whose only concern was for his pound of flesh.

The Social Gazette for December 2nd, 1899, reported the trial of three eighteen year old laundry girls who were being sued by their employer for leaving without notice. The defendants each earned six shillings weekly for a sixty-five hour stint. The plaintiff's solicitor declared that his client had suffered serious loss as a result of the girls' defection and wished an example to be made of them. In awarding the plaintiff a farthing damages with costs, the judge commented that had he paid his employees better the case might never have come into court adding that 'men have unions and associations for their protection; women appear to have none.' In point of reward there was little for a girl to choose between working in a laundry at a fraction over a penny an hour, and serving in a London chain of tea shops, having first worked a month for nothing while learning the trade.

Later her weekly wage could rise to twelve shillings — but from which she would have to pay for her own meals.

The middle aged woman — the widow or the deserted wife — could be at the mercy of the 'sweater' as she sought to maintain her children by making or finishing shirts. *The Social Gazette* for September 24th, 1898, was moved to reprint on its front page, under a banner headline 'The new echo of an old song', Thomas Hood's 'Song of the Shirt,' written forty-five years earlier for the Christmas number of *Punch*.

> Work — work — work
> Till the brain begins to swim;
> Work — work — work
> Till the eyes are heavy and dim!
> Seam, and gusset, and band,
> Band, and gusset, and seam
> Till over the buttons I fall asleep
> And sew them on in a dream.
> O men, with sisters dear!
> O men, with mothers and wives!
> It is not linen you're wearing out
> But human creatures' lives!
> Stitch — stitch — stitch
> In poverty, hunger and dirt,
> Sewing at once, with a double thread,
> A shroud as well as a shirt.

Prices for shirt making varied from one shilling to 2s. 4d. per dozen, according to size and quality, with the worker supplying her own thread and needles.

Similar conditions prevailed with the boxing and carding of hooks and eyes. When later the House of Commons set up a select committee on sweating, a chief factory inspector testified that in his area over a thousand women worked in this way at home, and the rate of pay varied from 8d. to 1s. 2d. per gross of cards, out of which the women had to

provide their own needles and thread. A woman could earn
from 2s. to 4s. 2d. per week, the latter figure being the
highest sum he had known.

Nor did old age bring a woman relief. Again *The Social
Gazette* was not behind hand in making known the facts.
The issue for September 15th, 1900, reported how an old lady
of sixty-nine spent the three shillings out-relief allowed her
by the Sleaford Board of Guardians — rent, 1s. per week;
bread 6d.; tea 2½d.; fire and light 7d.; flour 2½d.; dripping
2d.; milk and sugar 2d.; sundries 2d.

This state of affairs was not entirely the fault of the central
government. A month earlier, on August 18th, *The Social
Gazette* had quoted at length from a circular sent by Mr.
Chaplin, President of the Local Government Board, con-
cerning out-relief for 'the aged deserving poor.' The
President walked delicately but his meaning was plain.

> With regard to the treatment of the aged deserving
> poor . . . the Board is happy to think that it is the common
> practice of Boards of Guardians to grant outdoor relief
> in such cases, but they are afraid that too frequently such
> relief is not adequate in amount. They desire to press upon
> the Guardians that such relief should, when granted,
> always be adequate . . .

The Social Gazette had some justification for commenting
that it wished it could share the Board's hopes about outdoor relief — and then devastatingly quoted the current
practice of the Whitechapel Guardians. At their last meeting
Mr. Chaplin's circular had been read, after which the chairman had remarked that 'in the suggestions for the treatment
of the aged deserving poor, the Guardians had anticipated
all that had been proposed.' Yet the returns presented at
the same meeting showed that, of the 1,745 indoor paupers
in the area, only eleven were in receipt of outdoor relief, the
amount disbursed under this heading during the previous
week being £1. 3s. And, added the *Gazette*, the Whitechapel

Guardians have the reputation of being a liberally minded Board. We can assure Mr. Chaplin, the editorial continued, that his fears that 'such relief is not adequate in amount' are well grounded.

What Bramwell Booth thought of the position of women in England at the turn of the century can be read in his *Social Reparation*. Here are two abbreviated paragraphs:

A woman who is betrayed by a man has seldom any real redress. When he chooses he can cast her off without pity and without risk of punishment. His act may have deprived her of home, of livelihood, of all that makes life bright and possible. But her destroyer is free. No straw of responsibility, before the law of England, rests upon him. Villain as he knows himself to be, the law affixes no penalties. If the same man had so injured another man as to bring a tenth of the loss upon him that his conduct entailed on the woman, the state could have inflicted severe and humiliating punishment upon him. This is an injustice.

If a man hires a labourer to work for him, and promises to pay him certain money and give him certain food in return for his labour and then fails to do so, the labourer has the assistance of the law of the land in compelling his master to pay him his due. But if a man marries a woman and enters upon the obligations which the law lays down towards her, but then fails to keep his promises, the law is so weak that it is scarcely possible to compel him to fulfil his contract. What the law has given to the abused labourer in respect of his wages, it has withheld from the abused wife in respect of nearly everything which goes to make her life happy. This also is an injustice.

13

Let My People Go

When *In Darkest England* first appeared in October, 1890, William Booth's hopes for the success of his overseas colonies — in the plural — were as high as for any other part of his threefold plan. As he himself wrote: 'If this scheme proves the success we anticipate, the first colony will be the forerunner of similar communities elsewhere.' This was to be no blind shovelling of ill assorted batches of people from an island off the north-west coast of Europe to North America, or southern Africa, or Australia, where they would be left to fend for themselves in conditions whose novelty would but add to their difficulties.

The colonists themselves would be hand picked. First of all, they would be men and women of character. No use sending those, remarked William Booth, 'whose first enquiry on reaching land would be for the nearest whisky shop.' Australia and New Zealand were especially nervous lest this nineteenth-century migration would be a carbon copy of England's eighteenth-century deportations. Fears were loudly expressed that the arrival of thousands of the 'submerged' from Great Britain would submerge the honest toilers already living down under. The British tares would choke the good Australian wheat. 'For a fortnight' (wrote *The War Cry*) 'both islands — i.e. Australia and New Zealand — seem to have been alternately rocked between fervid wrath at the prospect of such an invasion, and a determination to smash the Cabinet for hoodwinking the public.' Had the fearful taken the trouble to read *In Darkest England* they would have noted that William Booth's faith

in his plans was coupled with his admission of the difficulties which 'barred the way to the emigration on any
considerable scale of the "submerged tenth".' He was not
for dumping England's rubbish on distant shores. His
chosen migrants would be twice blessed — profiting the
country to which they came and themselves by their coming.

He also gave thought to the means of their migration
and felt that 'we should be compelled to have a ship of our
own as soon as possible. A sailing vessel might be found the
best adapted for the work' — and he gave his reasons.

> Leaving out the question of time, which would be of
> very secondary importance with us, the construction of
> a sailing ship would afford more space for the accom-
> modation of emigrants and for industrial occupation, and
> would involve considerably less working expenses, beside
> costing very much less at the onset, even if we did not have
> one given us — which I think would be very probable.

The prospect lent wings to the imagination of its sixty
year old progenitor, as he continued:

> The captain, officers, and every member of the crew
> would be Salvationists, and all therefore alike interested
> in the enterprise. Moreover, the probabilities are that we
> should obtain the service of the ship's officers and crew
> in the most inexpensive manner, in harmony with the
> usages of the Army everywhere, men serving for love and
> not as a mere business . . . The effect produced by our
> ship cruising slowly southwards, testifying to the reality
> of a salvation for both worlds, calling at all convenient
> ports, would constitute a new kind of mission work, and
> draw out a large amount of practical sympathy.

There now only remained to settle the ship's destination,
and it was not William Booth's fault that his dreams were
never fully realised. For the remainder of his active life the

gospel of the overseas colony was never far from his lips. At one time New Zealand fully expected to host this new social venture. The Premier, John Ballance, the Minister of Lands, John McKenzie, and the Governor, the Earl of Onslow, favoured the proposal. After William Booth had expounded his scheme at a meeting in Christchurch in October, 1891, the Premier declared that he considered it the duty of the government to facilitate the proposal. Correspondence which revealed the government's willingness to ask Parliament to set aside ten thousand acres in the southern half of the North Island for the purpose of establishing a *Darkest England* colony was laid before the House of Representatives in July, 1892. Nevertheless there were those who continued to fear the entry of 'undesirable persons, the paupers and criminal scum of the alleys and byways of Great Britain.' In the end these unjustified fears prevailed.

There was a similar reaction in Australia, where William Booth was told that he should try his hand with the down and outs already in the country before 'emptying the refuse of Europe on to Australian shores.' He was not the man to take such a taunt lying down and *All the World* for December, 1893, reported the clearing of six hundred acres of virgin land for a farm at Pakenham, described as a village on the Gippsland railway line, thirty-eight miles out of Melbourne. But the spectre of a minor Botany Bay could not be laid. Though later on the West Australia parliament passed the necessary legislation to allow The Salvation Army to acquire a sufficiently large tract of land for the purpose of an overseas colony, and even though in the summer of 1900 the Kalgoorlie *Evening Star* reported that three hundred acres of land had already been ring barked, with thirty men at work vigorously clearing the bush, the old objections raised their head and the estate had to be adapted as a reformatory for young offenders.

Undismayed, William Booth had urged his cause in Canada. *The Social Gazette* for February 23rd, 1895, reported that at a reception given in his honour by the

Governor-General, the Earl of Aberdeen, William Booth asked that he might be granted 'a large section of land in the north-west on which he might settle graduates from the Salvation Army farm in England.' The upshot was that, later that same year, Colonel Stitt was seconded from the Hadleigh farm colony (where he was in charge) to visit Canada and report on how best this proposal might be implemented.

Meanwhile the Army leader in the United States, Frederick Booth-Tucker (who had married William Booth's second daughter, Emma), had coined the slogan: 'Place the landless man on the manless land,' and had commenced three farm colonies. It is not altogether clear whether these were to be linked with his father-in-law's overseas colony schemes, or were intended for the destitute of American cities only. In the event, however, the point did not arise.

The first was at Fort Romie in California where, in conjunction with the San Francisco Chamber of Commerce, $26,000 was paid for an area of land on which eighteen families from the city were settled. The scheme was hailed with expectations which, in the event, were not fully realised. The *New York Herald* described 'the possibilities of this colonisation scheme as boundless,' but the experiment broke down. The land was insufficiently irrigated. Seventeen of the eighteen families returned of their own accord to San Francisco. Booth-Tucker determined to profit by his mistakes. A more efficient irrigation system was installed and a fresh group of settlers secured — most of them unemployed but accustomed to country life. They were given a stake in the colony in that each was sold a plot under contract with payment spread over twenty years. Horses, stock and implements were also provided on the same terms.

The second, Fort Amity, was situated on prairie land in the valley of the Arkansas River. Poor families from Chicago were settled on twenty acre lots and Rider Haggard, when on a visit of inspection (see page 155) found 'a population of about 275 persons living in happiness, health and comfort, with a good prospect of becoming entirely independent.'

The third was the smaller colony of Fort Herrick, of 280 acres, so named because of the generosity of the donor, Myron T. Herrick of Cleveland. This included a home for inebriates but men came there as well who wished to learn farming, for such skills were in continuing demand. However, the overhead costs were higher than the returns warranted, and by 1908 The Salvation Army in the U.S.A. had ceased to be directly involved in any of these schemes.

William Booth continued to cherish his dreams and rely upon his friends. One of these was George Herring who had made a considerable fortune on the turf and who, though no orthodox believer, could be written down as one who loved his fellow men. But he died unexpectedly in November, 1906, and his passing ended the hopes which had been entertained for the newly introduced small holdings scheme at Boxted in Essex.

Another man, cast in the same giant mould, was Cecil Rhodes, and both he and Herring recognised in William Booth a personality of even greater stature still. Rhodes died in 1912, but nearly ten years earlier William Booth had taken him down to Hadleigh. On the return journey, at William Booth's suggestion, they had knelt to pray in the railway compartment in which they were travelling, after which Rhodes took his companion's hand and said: 'I hope you will continue to pray for me.'

The thousand acre farm given by Cecil Rhodes when he was Premier of the Cape Colony had convinced William Booth that Rhodesia was his land of promise. So now with redoubled vigour he personally canvassed virtually everyone whom he thought could aid him to establish his overseas colony there. In January, 1906, the British South Africa (the 'Chartered') Company promised him all the support in their power. How could he have foreseen that within two years he would be told that the Company could do nothing? A man of his word, he may have supposed that those on whom he counted would also swear to their own hurt, and change not.

In March of 1906 he saw Lord Rosebery who spoke of his personal interest in the Rhodesian proposals, and then he called on Lord Elgin, leaving a memorandum which the Colonial Secretary promised to consider. *The Mining World* announced that 'General Booth had his eyes on Rhodesia ... That the Rhodesian market should have been firmer at the very mention of a proposal to extend his work to that territory, shows the fascinating influence of his personality and the immense power for good which he wields over men and things.' He had already spent an hour and a quarter with the Prime Minister of that day, Sir Henry Campbell-Bannerman, who (so runs the journal note) 'did not make any promise of practical help in the shape of money for my scheme. However, he promised consideration, and I believe he will give it and do whatever can be done.'

A year elapsed — during which time William Booth visited Scandinavia, North America and Japan — before he was invited to call on Lord Rosebery again. He was prepared for bad news because the Army's solicitor had already received word that 'the Chartered Company could not carry out their intention to provide the money for his Rhodesian scheme.' Lord Rosebery made himself as agreeable to his visitor as he knew how, but the hard truth was that the Company was insolvent. William Booth repeated that his concern was for the unemployed in Britain. Rhodesia could provide work and home for them. Did his lordship think there was any hope of securing the government aid that had previously been refused? Memoranda outlining the scheme had been left with various government ministers.

This was a harkback to an earlier government initiative that, as a means of dealing with unemployment in Britain, Rider Haggard should report on the farm colonies for which the Army was responsible both in the homeland and North America. The terms of this mission were clear and plain.

It appears to the Secretary of State that, if these experiments are found to be successful, some analogous system, might with great advantage, be applied to transferring the urban populations of the United Kingdom to different parts of the British Empire.

In the event of 'the experiments made by The Salvation Army commending themselves to you,' Haggard was to include in his report —

any practical suggestions which may occur to you as to the means and methods whereby the example might best be turned to use in connexion with the projected transfer of urban populations of the United Kingdom to different parts of the British Empire.

With all diligence Rider Haggard presented a thoroughly objective report. There were warts on the American projects, but the response of the Canadian government more than compensated for these blemishes. Sir Wilfrid Laurier was ready to make an initial gift of 360 square miles of land for such a settlement and Earl Grey, the Governor General, expressed his confidence in the feasibility of such a scheme. All that was needed was the willingness of the Imperial Government — for this was still in the days of the British Empire — to guarantee a working loan.

The report was submitted to a government committee which took nearly twelve months to publish its findings. These were as disappointing as Mr. Walter Long's initial terms of enquiry had been promising. The committee's two main recommendations were that (*a*) no steps be taken by the government at present to further any scheme of colonisation but (*b*) a grant in aid could be given to the committees formed under the Unemployed Workmen Act for the purpose of emigration (i.e. as distinct from land settlement).

The first recommendation was based on the committee's judgment that 'there were serious objections to placing any such body as The Salvation Army in the position of managers of a colony dependent on money advanced by the Imperial Government.' The prospect of 'the return of any money advanced was uncertain, and the difficulty as to the selection of settlers serious, if not insurmountable.' In other words, the Imperial Government would not assist land settlement even within the British Empire, whatever any growing colony of British origin, and still under British authority, was willing to offer. This was as much a brush off for Canada as for William Booth.

About the second recommendation it should be noted — as this chapter subsequently shows — that the emigration schemes already operated by William Booth were proceeding without any government assistance whatever, and would continue to do so. He already knew more about emigration than all the committees formed under the Unemployed Workmen Act put together. He was grateful to all for their goodwill but indebted to none for their know-how. The truth was that however revered a figure William Booth might be in the public eye, The Salvation Army as such still stuck in the craw of the mandarins. And, as will be seen, in this particular matter William Booth got no further with the new Liberal government than with the old Conservative one.

To revert to the conversation with Lord Rosebery, his lordship suggested that his visitor should see the Chancellor of the Exchequer — which William Booth, ever hoping against hope, did the following day. Tea was served on the Terrace with personalities and photographers buzzing around. But for William Booth this was no social call. He wanted Lloyd George by himself in order to renew his plea for £100,000 for his dream settlement in Rhodesia. With suspicious alacrity the Chancellor took the seventy-seven year old leader from his own office to that of the Prime Minister.

'The General wants money for a colonisation scheme,' said Lloyd George.

'Gift or loan?' asked Mr. Asquith.

'Loan,' replied William Booth, 'but you will never ask for it back.'

'The General had better see Lord Crewe,' countered the Prime Minister — but the Colonial Secretary was occupied with a debate in the Lords, so William Booth returned to the House the following day. After the interview he noted that 'while very friendly, there was nothing in what the Colonial Secretary said, or in his manner of saying it, calculated to raise any expectations of success, or to strengthen any which I might have already entertained.'

By now William Booth was completely disillusioned and later wrote to Sir Abe Bailey:

Rhodesia is evidently gone ... I have heard such promises as Mr. Asquith seems to have hinted to you until their repetition only makes me sick at heart. They have ceased to have any influence upon my hopes or activities. The time extracted from my busy life, and the money withdrawn from our limited exchequer, and expended on Rhodesia during the last few years, I now regard as all but wasted ...

I have not changed my views that colonisation must be a natural outlet for the overplus population of this country, or that Rhodesia is the most likely country for such a scheme to be tried with the possibility of success, but ... that door at present is closed.

It was as well that William Booth had more than one shot in his locker. If he could not help the unemployed in one way, he would do so in another. His *Darkest England* scheme also included the 'multitudes of people all over the country who would be likely to emigrate could they be assisted to do so.' For their benefit an emigration board had been set up in London with Bramwell Booth at its head, and as early as 1885 a regular series of advertisements began to appear in the Army's press offering to assist intending emigrants in their choice of passages. A sample read:

EMIGRATION TO QUEENSLAND
Free passages are now granted to
female domestic servants
between the ages of seventeen and
thirty-five years, for whom there
is a great demand at high wages.
The rates ruling at the present
time are from 15s. to 30s. per
week for cooks; 12s. to 20s. for
laundresses; 10s. to 17s. for
housemaids and general servants,
with board and lodging.
For all further particulars,
apply W. H. Hawkins, the Shipping
Department, The Salvation Army ...

Small groups of men had already been transferred to selected openings in Canada and, thanks to the enterprise of James Hooker, a Salvationist builder and ironfounder in South Australia, a number of Salvation Army girls had found employment in that state. But the whole project took on new life after Commissioner David C. Lamb had visited Canada to enquire into the possibility of large scale emigration, and then returned to London as its director. The hallmark of this new scheme was its overall care for the migrant from the point of his (or her) departure to the point of final settlement.

Said William Booth:

By emigration I do not mean the imperfect and unsystematic thing which in the past has led to much disappointment and no little misery. For instance, no one can condemn more than I do the indiscriminate transfer of people from one country to another where, on landing, they are left in their ignorance to shift for themselves, thereby only too often becoming a sure prey to land sharks, and ultimately a source of perplexity and expense to the new community. Neither do I mean the exportation of the class more or less composed of the refuse of the community, whether they be vicious, criminal or wastrel.

As guidelines for his own officers, William Booth laid down that migration should be (1) helpful to the individual; (2) acceptable to the old land and (3) advantageous to the new country. Under such personalised care, it was only to be expected that migration became a happy experience for the emigrants themselves and of benefit to the country of their adoption.

These practical plans aroused nationwide interest and on Monday, January 23rd, 1905, the first fourteen of fifty families sponsored by *The Daily Telegraph* shilling fund, left West Ham for Canada. Most of these migrants had been unemployed. A typical story was that of a dock labourer who had been compelled to sell his furniture piece by piece in order to keep his family alive until he was reduced to one room with one table, one bed and two chairs. Those hopeless days were now behind him for he, like every other emigrant breadwinner, was either going to an assured situation, or would be cared for until suitable work had been found.

In the following April another three hundred migrants left for Canada, including twenty-four from the Poplar farm colony at Laindon, ten from the Marylebone workhouse, and thirty-one from the Hadleigh farm colony. Will Crooks, then M.P. for Woolwich, addressed the emigrants: 'You must all be grateful for the way in which plans have been carried out for you to leave the old world, which perhaps has been none too kind to you, and for sending you to the new world. Commissioner Lamb has taken considerable trouble to make every arrangement for your comfort.'

Before that same month was out a further thousand migrants had sailed from Liverpool on board the 'Vancouver' which had been specially chartered for this purpose. Only seventeen per cent of this giant party had shared any previous association with The Salvation Army. Thirty-three per cent were members of the Anglican communion. Ten per cent had no regular church affiliation at all. The rest belonged to various other churches — Protestant and Roman Catholic alike — in the United Kingdom. About half of the company had a definite destination in view; the others would consult during the voyage with the Army's Canadian representative on board who had details of four hundred possible openings with him.

Other frequent sailings followed and, by the summer of 1908, more than 36,000 migrants had travelled under the auspices of the Army, and the blessing of the Canadian authorities, to the land of their adoption. As Earl Grey cabled to the company on board the S.S. 'Southwark': 'You are heartily welcome, as will be others of the same kind, for whom there is plenty of room.'

The Empire Settlement Act of 1922 stimulated the flow of migrants still further, except that between the wars many leaving Britain began to show a preference for Australia. With the approval of the British and Commonwealth governments, the White Star liner 'Vedic' was chartered for an autumn sailing in 1927 — and again in 1928 and 1929. About this impressive piece of social enterprise, the Rt. Hon. Stanley Bruce, Prime Minister of Australia, said: 'We in Australia know the Army as the only non-sectarian religious organisation which is helping in the great task of overseas settlement. Its methods are an admirable combination of philanthropy and efficient business dealing. Its aftercare of migrants is marked by a sympathetic human touch.'

Between the wars the New Zealand government also set up a department of immigration and, in the first two years of its existence, upwards of a thousand men and women who took advantage of the government scheme were found employment by the Army. During the same period in New Zealand, and in Australia after the Second World War, literally hundreds of lads were received from Great Britain and placed on farms in both countries, after having been given preliminary training.

Migration on this scale is no longer the vogue, but it can be said that, by the outbreak of the Second World War, more than a quarter of a million people had been given a new life in new surroundings. Less than fifteen per cent of this number had enjoyed previous Salvation Army affiliation, and less than one per cent of the grand total turned out to be failures. This can therefore be legitimately described as a disinterested social undertaking which, motivated by Christian concern as were all William Booth's endeavours, proved of economic benefit to the unemployed in Britain and provided the Dominions of that day with an increased work force as well.

14

Nations Shall Call Him Blessed

As the lamps of Europe were beginning to flicker ominously, William Booth was reaching the end of his more than eighty crowded years. Until his final public appearance in the Royal Albert Hall on May 9th, 1912, he had maintained the liveliest interest in the multifarious needs of the world which, as was his wont, he interpreted in terms of individual men and women.

His first concern had always been for their spiritual and moral welfare, though the bread and butter question was never far from his heart and mind. His spirit still longed to serve them for he had always been on their side. Even when blind he could hardly eat his own breakfast sometimes for thinking of the small children in dockland, hungry because of a labour dispute. But the flesh was weak. In the Royal Albert Hall he had described himself as 'going into dry dock for repairs.' To his diary he confided that he often felt like 'a worn out garment.' He was sightless. His memory was failing. A walk in the garden, varied by a short motor run in the countryside, marked the ever diminishing limits of his strength. These were not the conditions for recollecting in tranquillity the work which he had been enabled to do. His restless spirit forbade him such an emotional luxury, though he could have comforted himself with the truth that some of his social experiments, once despised and almost rejected of men, had now been adopted as practical politics.

Labour exchanges were one of these. A solitary office for the voluntary registration of the unemployed had been opened in Chelsea in 1887, but this was something of a

loner. However, even before *In Darkest England* was published, William Booth had opened his first labour bureau
on June 16th, 1890, housed in an Upper Thames Street
office to begin with, and then transferred to 272, Whitechapel Road. Advertisements in the Army's press catalogued
the work of the bureau in the most liberal terms.

Employment and advertising in all
its branches
Board carrying   Window cleaning
Circular folding
Envelope addressing   Ticket writing
Messengers in city, suburbs and provinces
Artistic signboards painted
Fascias and signboards
renovated — a speciality
Special terms for permanent
posters in central positions
Contracts made at favourable prices
Workmen supplied   Large numbers always on hand

'I propose,' William Booth had written, 'to establish
registers which will enable us to lay our hands at a moment's
notice upon all the unemployed men in a district in any
particular trade. In this way we will become the universal
intermediary between those who have no employment and
those who want workmen.'

Within the first fifteen weeks of the bureau's existence
there were 2,670 applications for employment, of which 146
were found permanent work, 223 temporary employment,
while 146 were taken in at the sheltered workshop (or
elevator) in Hanbury Street. A tiny drop in an immense
ocean! Without doubt! But William Booth was never the
man to despise the day of small things. For in the year
ended September 30th, 1903, permanent or temporary work
was found for 4,862 out of 10,056 applications. As time went
on the number of those seeking work did not decline, though

the ratio of those for whom employment was found fell slightly. For example, for the three months ended June 30th, 1908, there were 3,816 applicants and work was found for 1,525.

It has to be remembered that even the best intentioned were working somewhat in the dark. In November of that same year the Prime Minister had to agree in the House that 'the information at the disposal of H.M. government does not enable them to give any trustworthy information concerning the number of unemployed.' 'Such helplessness,' commented *The Social Gazette*, 'would be farcical were it not tragic. We can tell how many lunatics, criminals and paupers there are in the country, but not the number of our fellow men and women in danger of falling victims to starvation ... The need of a measure for the compulsory registration of the unemployed could not be more powerfully presented.'

Even as the *Gazette* fulminated, labour exchanges were on their way. When Mr. Winston Churchill became President of the Board of Trade in the spring of 1908, he brought William (later Lord) Beveridge into his department. The newcomer, who had already made a name with his study: *Unemployment: a Problem of Industry*, helped to prepare the case for labour exchanges for the consideration of the Cabinet. The required bill passed through all its parliamentary stages in the summer of 1909, and the initial eighty-three centres opened their doors on February 1st, 1910 — nearly twenty years after William Booth had set up his first modest office for the same purpose in Upper Thames Street.

Once again Christian initiative had prepared the way for public action, and *The Social Gazette* for February 12th, 1910, described in a two column spread the benefits which would now accrue.

Henceforth the problem of unemployment will, to a large extent, be dealt with in an organised manner. It is true that these institutions will not make work; but the honest and capable workman will be spared the weary tramp from town to town in search of employment. When seeking for a job he will register his name, trade and address at the nearest bureau. If there is a demand in the district for such work as he is capable of doing, he will at once be sent to the employer with his card of reference . . . All the exchanges will be linked up and will report to each other the demand and the class of workers required.

Allied to this new provision was the National Insurance Act which came into operation on July 15th, 1912. Men and women between sixteen and seventy years of age, whose wages did not exceed £160 per annum, were to select a 'friendly' or 'approved' society of which they would become members and through which the Act would operate. William Booth had his agency ready. This new member of his steadily growing band of social services was the Reliance Benefit Society.

He could also have comforted himself that his unwearying campaign against the outworking of the Poor Law Amendment Act of 1834 was bearing fruit — if not an hundredfold, at least a very satisfying sixtyfold. The walls of such a well entrenched Jericho do not collapse when the trumpets of righteousness have sounded round about them seven times; seventy times seven is frequently nearer the mark. The leader in No. 5 of the *Darkest England Gazette* (which had preceded *The Social Gazette*) had as its text the 'ingrained detestation in the soul of every Englishman of the entire pauper system.' The writer was pardonably carried away by his theme. Not 'every Englishman' detested the system. There were those who upheld it — for example, the stalwarts of the Charity Organisation Society such as C. S. Loch, Mrs. Bosanquet and Octavia Hill who sat on, and testified before, the Poor Law Commission which deliberated from December, 1905 to February, 1909. It was their view that 'a general responsibility for providing work for the unemployed was not to be accepted by any public body.'

Then by whom, William Booth would have asked. In their *The Prevention of Destitution* (published by Longmans, Green & Co. in 1911) the discerning Sidney and Beatrice Webb noted that —

... the alliance between a discriminating philanthropy and a deterrent Poor Law, which had first seemed so plausible, found its determined opponent in General Booth and The Salvation Army. Revealing to an astonished world the extent of the mass of chronic destitution in our large towns ... he convinced public opinion that the 'deterrent' regime of the Poor Law had so far succeeded, or so far failed — whichever view might be preferred — as to leave outside its scope hundreds of thousands of persons whose destitution was real enough to become a social danger ... *In Darkest England* showed that both the Poor Law and charity had failed to prevent, or even to relieve, destitution.

But William Booth offered more than negative criticism of an existing system. Nor were his alternatives merely set down in writing. Much of his *Darkest England* scheme had been in actual practice for nearly as long as it had been on paper, so it was with a very clear conscience that he could respond to an invitation from the British Institute of Social Service to contribute a paper on Poor Law Reform which appeared in 1908 in their journal *Progress*.

'It will be generally acknowledged,' he began, 'that the methods of our present Poor Law have largely failed to restore to a state of manly efficiency the lowest grades of our social life. In order to remedy this, many of the punitive arrangements for dealing with paupers, vagrants, incorrigibles and criminals should give place to more rational and reformatory methods.' This led him to plead for a more careful classification of human disorders in order that the remedies suggested should accomplish their purpose. What follows is a heavily abridged summary of his proposals which — with room for further sub-divisions — he set out under four main headings. These four dealt in turn with (1) the incapacitated, (2) the confirmed vagrant or criminal, (3) the unemployed and (4) the child.

(1) The incapacitated would include all who were incapable of remunerative work because of (a) age, (b) physical unfitness, (c) mental feebleness and (d) sickness. Old Age pensions which the State was about to provide would help to relieve the necessities of the aged poor.

The physically unfit could be retrained in such light employment as might suit their condition. The feeble-minded, if not in the care of an appropriate family guardian, should be placed in a friendly setting as much like home as possible and as far removed as possible from the setting of the workhouse. The sick would be a first charge upon the nation. A national health authority would take the initiative and, instead of waiting for the needy sick to report their illness, would visit and prescribe as might be required.

(2) For the second group, consideration could be given to the establishment of compulsory farm or labour colonies. A vagrant might enter such a colony voluntarily or, if incorrigible, could be sentenced after due trial to a period in such a colony, as a convicted criminal is now sent to prison. The medicine of useful labour would be far more beneficial than the poison of forced and unprofitable idleness in which a prisoner was a total charge upon the state.

(3) For the unemployed there should be compulsory registration, with similar action required of employers with regard to present or future labour vacancies. At present the absence of any national labour exchanges meant that the country simply muddled through periods of normal or abnormal distress. (This was written before

the bill of 1909). Colonisation by emigration would also play a valuable part in providing work for the unemployed.

(4) Nothing has given me greater pleasure (William Booth concluded) than the progress which has been made towards the humane treatment of the homeless or parentless child. All future schemes should be so implemented that no child grows up bearing an odious brand.

'Finally,' the paper ended, 'I would not disguise the fact that I attach far more importance to the reform of the man than the reform of the law. The problem of problems lies here in a nutshell.'

Such proposals plainly bear the mark of their date, but they must have sounded revolutionary at the time. Yet remembering that they were put forward only seventy years ago, it is remarkable how many of them have come to pass. A national health scheme, universal unemployment insurance, the open prison, equal educational opportunities for every child were all here in embryo.

William Booth could also have comforted himself that, although no longer able to lead his Army as actively as had been his habit, his officers and soldiers were as loyal to their calling and as compassionate in its exercise as ever.

Of the first there was no possible doubt. Only weeks before his passing the corps officer at Scunthorpe was released from Lincoln prison after serving seven days in the third division (which included oakum picking) for holding a religious service which was alleged to have caused a street obstruction. As for the second, the two major industrial disputes which worked such havoc in the early spring and late summer of 1912 — the miners' and the dockers' strikes respectively — provided his people with ample opportunity to manifest their sense of compassion.

To quote once more an undeniable authority upon the human scene, this was what commended the officer corps of The Salvation Army to Beatrice Webb. 'Salvation Army officers' (she wrote) 'owe their power, and the enormous respect which people have for them, to their vows of poverty and obedience.' Poverty is a comparative term. Perhaps some such clumsier phrase as 'frugal life style' might be more accurate; the principle that a man should not waste on his own personal fancy that which could satisfy the need of his less privileged neighbour.

At any rate there was the widest possible scope for demonstrating this virtue during the prolonged mining dispute which affected every coalfield in Great Britain and which was ended only by the passing of the Minimum Wage Bill. The near starvation conditions which prevailed in many areas long outlasted the return to work. 'We have no desire to represent the miners as faultless,' said the Army's press at the time, 'but the idea that they are a quarrelsome set of men, always at loggerheads with their employers, is as false as the impression fostered by pictures in the cheap papers that they are everlastingly pigeon flying, beer drinking and football playing . . . The Army has good reason to know this . . . for many of them are loyal Salvationists.'

A double column heading: 'Plight of the Poor' prefaced an appeal from William Booth himself.

> The suffering among the decent poor consequent upon the present sad industrial strife has now become a most serious matter . . . Every day, indeed, every hour that now passes widens the sad field of hunger and misery . . . The reports of my officers in many parts of the country tell the same story of privation and sorrow which must inevitably be aggravated during the next few days. It is also evident that even when the strike ceases there must be further suffering ere wages are forthcoming . . . Please help me to enable my devoted workers to set about meeting pressing necessities . . . food and fuel.

Reports followed in a flood, of 450 people being fed daily at Morley; of 300 being given a regular meal of soup and bread in Nottingham; of *The Daily Mirror* financing in

London the distribution of fresh milk among nursing mothers and young children; of 850 children at Ashton-under-Lyne being fed each day in the Army hall; of 5,000 meals being provided in less than a week in Hamilton; of 500 meals provided seven days a week at Longton; of regular food distribution in such areas of Glasgow as Parkhead, Shettleston and Garngad; of queues for coal forming up in East London outside distribution centres which had been set up in Hanbury Street and Mare Street.

Before the summer was out the same sorry scenes were repeated in London's dockland. On both sides of the Thames bread tickets and grocery tickets were the order of the day. As the school holidays were still on, arrangements were made for parties of 250 children at a time to be taken from Poplar, Canning Town, Silvertown and West Ham for a fortnight to Thundersley where, in the grounds of Victoria House, they were given a free holiday with abundant food and fun. But, with the dock dispute barely ended, William Booth's earthly service ended also.

There had never been any doubt as to where his sympathies lay. To paraphrase St. Paul somewhat, to the underdog he became an underdog. Charles Williams noted this in his *The Descent of the Dove*. Such bodies as the Poor Clares and The Salvation Army (he wrote) were not regarded 'in the eyes of the masses of men (as) the great support of the dominant social order.' This could have been why William Booth's last interview with Mr. Churchill, then Home Secretary, had to do with prison reform. To the end he wanted to help the man at the bottom of the heap. Not without reason did Harold Begbie quote some words of Tagore on the flyleaf of his two volume biography. 'Here is thy footstool and there rest thy feet where live the poorest, and lowliest, and lost.'

15

A Memorial unto all Generations

William Booth left a twofold legacy which is still bearing generous interest and will continue to do so for the foreseeable future. Part of his bequest is that by his own courageous experimentation — undertaken not infrequently, as has been seen, in face of public opposition, bureaucratic obstruction as well as personal vilification — he helped to shape a nation's thinking concerning things to come. In a phrase used in parliament, he 'pioneered ahead of the state,' and this he did outside as well as inside Britain.

The place of voluntary societies within the welfare state is now as certain as anything can be in a world of uncertainties. The Nathan Report was more than justified in observing that 'so far from voluntary action being dried up by the extension of the social services, greater and greater demands are being made upon it. We believe, indeed, that the democratic state, as we know it, could hardly function effectively ... without such channels for, and demands upon, voluntary service.'

For instance, in mid-summer, 1977, *The Times* reported that the public benches on or near the Thames Embankment were still full overnight. As many people still sleep rough as can be housed in the existing official reception centres for homeless men. That is one reason why The Salvation Army continues to be the largest single voluntary provider of sleeping accommodation for such men in Britain, having increased its share of the overall provision from 21 per cent in 1965 to 24 per cent in 1972. Such voluntary service is plainly an indispensable adjunct to the machinery of the State.

As has already been noted, it was such action — personified by William Booth — which provided a pilot scheme for the registration of the unemployed twenty years before the State set up its own exchanges. Similarly, in his *Poor Man's Lawyer* can be seen the precursor of the present citizens' advice bureau. Some of the answers given by the 'lawyer' — which must be read in the light of prevailing conditions — indicate the nature of the unsolicited enquiries:

> You can recover your week's wages. Take out a summons at the nearest police court.
>
> You cannot compel your husband to maintain you while you are living apart.
>
> We are sorry to say that both rabbit coursing, hare coursing and stag hunting are still legalised cruelties.
>
> It all depends what you were dismissed for. Send full particulars and do not hide anything.
>
> What was your wage and how were you paid — by the hour, day or week? If by the latter, you are entitled to a week's notice, or to a week's wages in lieu of notice.
>
> You cannot sue Tattersall's as the law still allows bets to be booked so long as no money changes hands on the premises.

'Farthing breakfasts' were a forerunner of the present school meals system. At the beginning of 1894 the *Darkest England Gazette* carried a two page report describing twenty thousand children, living mainly in what would now be called the Inner London area, receiving for a farthing a large mug of coffee or cocoa and a substantial bread roll before going to school. Similar cheap breakfasts were provided at other urban centres. The alternative was to creep hungrily — as well as unwillingly — to school, a state of

body and mind reflected in the child's work in the class
room.*

The care of the aged now figures prominently in every
political programme. Provision for senior citizens is now
undertaken by most local authorities, but Commissioner
Adelaide Cox, who became a Salvation Army officer in
1881, was also for twenty years a member of the Hackney
Board of Guardians. 'Nothing seemed to me so tragic,' she
wrote, 'as the plight of the respectable aged who came before
our Board ... With the utmost self-denial they could not
make ends meet because they had no one to assist them with
the rent. At the same time the law prevented monetary
grants being made for that purpose; a Board of Guardians
could help only by supplying "an order for the house" —
the workhouse ... To them that sounded like the death
knell.' The upshot was that in November, 1910, 'a small
house on the borders of Epping Forest was secured for an
eventide home for ten old age pensioners.'

The Salvation Army in Norway began to house senior
citizens in 1909, but Australia began earlier still — at
Pakenham (Victoria) in 1901 and a year later in Manly
(New South Wales). All this prepared the way for similar
provision — both voluntary and statutory — in many other
parts of the world, and today in Britain the Army still takes
good care of more than two thousand senior citizens a number of them married couples.

The other part of William Booth's legacy is that he raised
up, under God, a body of trained men and women who
learned to express their love for God in a concern for their
neighbour, and their like-minded descendants are with us
to this day. For them 'informed goodwill is the light of the
world.' One of the regrettable limitations of this paperback
is that lack of space prevents any adequate description of
their global activities which transcend all barriers, whether

---

* The writer can recall his officer parents supervising such a winter's
feeding programme in the Scottish seaport to which they had been
appointed prior to the First World War.

of colour, or culture, or class. Thanks to the eternally present spirit of Christ in the heart of His servants, differences of race or language cannot limit the outworking of their concern. The work which William Booth commenced has never been short of examples of this.

In the opening decade of the present century the traditional home industries in India were dying. For instance, the village weaver who laboured under his own roof was being ruthlessly undercut by the city factories. His primitive machine could not compete with the power-driven loom. To imperial India came a North London boy who possessed a flair for machinery but who, at the age of thirty-six, became a Salvation Army officer. Frank Maxwell was no public speaker but he had a lively mind, an agile pair of hands and a compassionate heart. In the providence of God he was confronted by the plight of the village weaver. It did not need a genius to see that his machine was hopelessly outdated, but it did need more than a touch of genius to construct, out of wood from packing cases, a simple handloom with automatic action which took the first prize in the spring of 1906 at the Ahmedabad agricultural and industrial exhibition.

In the following year Maxwell took the first prize in a three days' open competition in Calcutta. Prizes now became a habit with him. From 1908 to 1911 he was awarded either the gold, silver or bronze medal at exhibitions in Madras, Mysore, Nagpur, Lahore and Allahabad. Orders for his automatic loom began to reach him from all parts of the subcontinent. These were made of Burma teak wood, light but strong, durable but easy to work. A co-operative society was formed to enable villagers to instal one of these low-priced looms in their own home. The British Raj opened a weaving school in Ludhiana equipped with Maxwell's looms. He made no personal profit out of his invention for the patent had been passed over to The Salvation Army, but more than eight hundred of them were manufactured in the first five years.

Perhaps his greatest moment was when Gandhi sought him out and the two men met in the ashram at Ahmedabad. Maxwell's loom seemed the answer to the Mahatma's prayer. This was just what he needed to transform his *swadeshi* (home industry) movement from an ideal to a nationwide possibility. But the Indian leader had second thoughts.

'No, I can't do it. Ours is an all-India movement, and I couldn't use a loom invented by a white man.'

'But Gandhiji,' was the quiet reply, 'the looms are made in our factory in India by Indian craftsmen. I only oversight their work.'

'All the same,' answered Gandhi, 'my movement could not adopt your loom. You see the cotton is grown by us, spun by us, woven by us . . .'

Maxwell was slow of speech but not dull of eye. He remembered what he had seen in a corner of the ashram and interrupted: 'And sewn — on a Singer sewing machine.' Before long, Maxwell's biographer has written, 'hundreds of Gandhi's followers were using the simple automatic handloom which was one of this Army officer's greatest contributions to the welfare of the people of India.'

By contrast, take the closing of the penal settlement in French Guiana, popularly though incorrectly known as Devil's Island — a labour which was even more prolonged yet equally disinterested.

'The Bagne' — as the convicts called it — dated from 1852 when criminals from metropolitan France were transported across the Atlantic to a reception centre seventy-five miles up the Maroni River which then formed the boundary between Dutch and French Guiana. From there they were sent to work in various labour camps from which escape was virtually impossible. Five miles off the coast lay three small islands, one of which was Devil's Island, made notorious by the presence of the unfortunate Dreyfus. The sharks were the warders. But most unfortunate of all were the *libérés* — men who had served their prison sentence but

who could not leave Guiana. Under an iniquitous rule
anyone sentenced to a seven year term or less had to remain
in the colony for a further equal number of years. Those
who were sentenced to eight years or more had to remain in
the colony for life. Most men, when they were entitled to
leave, lacked the money to pay their fare home.

The truth about conditions in the penal settlement had
filtered through to France, but it was not until a twenty-
seven year old Salvation Army officer, Charles Péan, visited
Guiana in 1928 and returned to describe the prevailing
system as 'white slavery' that remedial action began — and
then only slowly. Péan's report was presented by his Army
leader to the Minister for the Colonies in 1933, but 1938
had begun before official consent was given for him, with
half-a-dozen other Salvation Army officers, to commence
their merciful work. A hostel and workshop for the *libérés*
was opened in Cayenne and St. Laurent. Ground was
secured for a farm at Montjoly. A scheme was started
whereby any *libéré* who had served his *doublage* and who
genuinely desired to return home was provided with free
bed and board at the hostel and, in addition to a regular
gratuity for work done, also received a voucher which could
be deposited, in whole or in part, with the Army against his
fare home.

The first shipload of repatriates arrived in St. Nazaire
early in 1936 but, when the second world war broke out,
regular communication between Paris and Guiana ceased.
The internal dissensions which sadly afflicted the French
people at home were reflected overseas. Not until after the
armistice could Péan cross the Atlantic again though,
by this time, the Minister of Justice had allocated a sum
sufficient to cover the repatriation of the remaining two
thousand *libérés*. By August, 1953, the *Bagne* was no
more. It was twenty-five years since Péan first sighted its
shores.

Such a work of prison reform is public and dramatic.
Other endeavours in the same field are often unheralded and

unsung — as with the present provision in Great Britain of bail hostels.

The first such hostel was inspired and financed by the Xenia Field Foundation and opened in November, 1971, for an experimental period of three years as part of Booth House. (This was a social service complex in the Whitechapel Road, London, opened by H.M. Queen Elizabeth II in the spring of 1968.) The need for such provision was evidenced by the fact that in 1969 44,267 untried persons were sent to prison in England and Wales — that is, they were remanded in custody. Of this number, 2,079 were subsequently found not guilty, and another 22,233 were not given a custodial sentence — that is, they were either placed on probation, or fined, or given a suspended sentence, or conditionally discharged. In other words, over fifty per cent of those who had been remanded in custody were not thereafter imprisoned.

A study by the Cobden Trust of a thousand hearings showed that an accused person — irrespective of his past record or present offence — was usually remanded in custody if he was of 'no fixed abode.' Finally there was need for an alternative to such procedure, and repeated approaches by Mrs. Xenia Field to the Home Office finally secured government willingness for a privately financed and administered experiment to be undertaken. After further consultation with the Inner London Probation and After Care Service, the Army agreed to provide such accommodation —

(1) to enable the courts to release on bail men charged with comparatively minor offences who would otherwise be remanded in custody, mainly because they had no fixed abode; and
(2) to afford the defendants such help as might be necessary to make constructive use of the remand period.

Those whom the scheme was intended to help were male

first offenders of seventeen years of age and over who had appeared in a magistrate's court, but who were neither addicted to drugs nor drink, were not disturbingly mentally sick, and who had no record of sexual offences against children. The current practice with any who accept the Army's bail hostel in lieu of a prison remand is to be interviewed on arrival, given the key of his single room and, where needful, helped with toilet necessities and clothing. If employed, he will pay £10.25 (at current rates) for bed and breakfast. If unemployed, he will visit the local office of the Department of Employment in order to register and then visit the Department of Health and Social Security who will meet the cost of his full board while he is unemployed and provide him with £4.10 pocket money per week.

A Home Office research unit made a study of the experiment which was published by H.M. Stationery Office in 1975. Meanwhile as section 53 of the Criminal Justice Act of 1972 empowered the Home Secretary to finance bail hostels, government plans are now afoot to make such provision available, and The Salvation Army is planning similar hostels in Cardiff, Coventry and Darlington. In this way a young man can avoid the shock of a custodial remand and its consequent stigma. Further, the bail hostel allows a man to continue in his current employment or, if he is unemployed, to try to find work. Nor is he cut off, as he would be in prison, from his family and friends.

Up to the time of writing over five hundred men have been accommodated at the Field Wing Bail Hostel and it has been — so declared the officer associated with the experiment from the start — 'a place of positive good, where men are in a position to be influenced for Christ, beside receiving the minimal advantage of food and shelter'*.

Whitechapel may be deemed stony soil for the Christian

---

* The above material is taken from a study by Captain Trevor Tribble, until August, 1977, Director of the Booth House/Victoria Home complex, and currently in charge of the Men's Social Services in Scotland.

gospel, but it is not without significance that the Field Wing
Bail Hostel is within sight of the spot where William Booth
began his life's work in 1865. But if his men and women
can thole the long travail where planning and prayer play
their complementary parts, they are equally ready to grapple
with the sudden havoc caused by natural disaster or human
error. Three brief examples from the present decade will
conclude this study.

The early news bulletins on the Australian radio on
Christmas day, 1974, did nothing more than announce that
a disaster of unknown severity had befallen Darwin in the
Northern Territory. By the time Christmas dinner — that
unique compound 'down under' of a hot meal and ice-cold
drinks — had been served, it was clear that cyclone 'Tracy'
had devastated Darwin. Christmas day or not, the departmental heads of The Salvation Army's territorial headquarters in Melbourne were called to 69, Bourke Street, and
all divisional headquarters were alerted. All commercial
air traffic in and out of Darwin had been suspended so that
representatives of many interests were clamouring for a
seat when it was known that there was to be a flight there
via Brisbane. The one vacant place left was given to The
Salvation Army.

When Commissioner H. J. Warren, the then leader of the
Southern Territory (which, despite the logic of geography,
includes Darwin) arrived in Brisbane, the airport manager
there spoke of his fears that, should there be a flood of
evacuees, the necessary supplies of medicine, food and
clothing — not to mention living accommodation — might
not be available. Although an evacuation order had not yet
been issued, the manager's foresight enabled Army leaders
in Sydney as well as Melbourne to be warned of what might
be expected of them.

Twelve hours after leaving the Victorian capital, Commissioner Warren set down on the Darwin runway, where
only damaged aircraft and deserted hangars were to be seen.
Making for the perimeter, he identified the Army's Cessna

182 — used by the flying service — by the Red Shield
emblem on its torn fuselage, and then set out along the
highway, littered with wreckage, to walk into the city. A
lone vehicle with a lone driver pulled up at the sight of the
lone wearer of Salvation Army uniform, and the two men
made their way together to what was left of Mitchell Street
— site of the former Army hall and officers' quarters.

Here were found a handful of local Salvationists together
with Captain and Mrs. Alan Watson (the corps officers)
and Captain and Mrs. Hilton Morris (of the flying service).
Greetings had hardly been exchanged and prayers of thanksgiving for preservation said when word came that a priest
was needed — whereupon the Commissioner was taken to
the damaged hospital to pray with a dying man, every
member of whose family had suffered injury of one kind or
another. Midnight saw a conference convened under the
Civilian Director General, Major-General Alan Stretton,
who had flown in from Canberra, and the order was issued
that the evacuation of all civilians from the disaster area
was to proceed with all speed.

Within four days a hundred Salvationists of various ranks
and varied skills, armed with entry permits, arrived to assist
in this operation. As all power and water supplies had
broken down, the city was rapidly becoming uninhabitable,
so the arrival of six generators as part of the first Salvation
Army relief consignment was more than welcome. A group
of Salvationist tradesmen in Perth chartered their own plane
and, bringing their tools with them, began working on
emergency repairs. Others joined convoys from Mount Isa
and Alice Springs and promptly set to work on the airlift
which moved over 25,000 people in five days. The greater
part of this effort was serviced by Salvationists who staffed
the temporary canteens, manned the ticket counters, served
as baggage handlers, helped harassed mothers, looked after
tired children, even acted as air hostesses, as well as supervised the distribution of goods from the immense super-
market which became at night their improvised dormitory.

At the various points of arrival the evacuees were met by other organised groups of Salvationists who again over-sighted the movement of luggage, and saw to it that no one was stranded at any airport with nowhere to go or, having an address, lacked the means of reaching it.

This Australian operation could be regarded as feasible in a community where another cobber's troubles have long been accepted as one's own. But such an explanation does not cover the response to human need in Guatemala.

At 3 a.m. on Monday, February 4th, 1976, an earthquake measuring 7·5 on the Richter scale shook the district of Chimaltenango, and was followed two days later by a second major shock registering 6·0. Within forty-eight hours of the first, and within a few hours of the second, Brigadier Newton McClements had flown in from Kingston, Jamaica and unannounced, but not unwelcome, set up a relief centre in Guatemala City. He was speedily joined by bi-lingual officers from Mexico and the United States, and in a matter of days relief supplies began to arrive. The Brigadier had to return to his duties in Kingston, but not before an experienced team of officers and Salvationist volunteers — many of whom had served in the Honduras hurricane in 1974 and the earthquake in northern Peru in 1970* — were at work.

Thanks to the generosity of the principal American air-lines, a major part of their free cargo space out of New York, San Francisco, Houston and Miami was placed at the Army's disposal. Food, bedding, tents, clothing and medical supplies were flown into Guatemala City airport, while heavier items were brought into the country through Port San José and Port Santa Tomas. Though there is a sad similarity about these relief operations, a blanket is always more than just a blanket. A tent means a new home, even if temporary. A tin of pork and beans is a feast to a starving man.

*See *The clock stopped at 3.25* by Winifred O. Gearing (Daniels Publishers, Orlando, Florida).

To prevent overlapping, the President of the Republic assigned specific areas to specific groups and the Army was given the city and neighbourhood of Tecpan, some seventy miles north-west of the capital. Three thousand of the twenty-five thousand population had died; another seven thousand had been injured; the city itself had been flattened. Wholesale reconstruction, not merely temporary relief, was required.

Already a hospitality centre had been set up in the airport which served the capital, and a missing persons enquiry office had been opened to assist relatives and friends at home and overseas who were seeking news of their loved ones in the disaster area. Overseas enquiries were facilitated by the Radio Relay League linking Guatemala City with Atlanta. By the beginning of March a medical clinic had also been set up amid the ruins of Tecpan, and this served the local population until more adequate hospital facilities were restored in August.

Meanwhile plans were drawn up for a prototype house which could be erected both speedily and economically and yet prove sufficient for normal family life. A cement block-making plant was shipped in from San Francisco. Herbert Phillips, a Salvationist volunteer of the Phillips Truss Company in Anniston, Alabama, set up a pre-fabricated shop where gable ends, window fittings and door frames could be manufactured as near as possible to the actual building sites selected by the Tecpan authorities. Church World Service helped with the supply of lamina roofing. Construction work was financed not only through Salvation Army appeals but by contributions from the Evangelical Alliance, the 'Wild Geese' (a radio and television programme operated by the Dutch Protestant churches), 'Help the Aged' and 'Action in Distress' in London. U.S.A.I.D. assisted with the provision of tools and the transport of construction materials, the whole effort being coordinated by The Salvation Army as the overall authority responsible for the area.

A public welcome was accorded to Commissioner Ernest Holz when he arrived in Tecpan on August 6th, 1976, to present the first thirty-one completed homes to the people of the city. The total scheme provided for five hundred houses altogether. In addition, a pre-fabricated building was erected as a community and education centre, and the cement plant was kept in operation to assist with the erection of the new hospital.

Finally, the public impact of any disaster is usually in direct proportion to its proximity. For that reason the Moorgate calamity of February 28th, 1975, was felt throughout the British Isles. The 8.46 a.m. Northern Line six car train failed to stop at platform nine and crashed at speed into the solid concrete wall at the end of the tunnel. 118 feet of train were telescoped into 66 feet of space. Forty-three commutors died; eighty-six were injured; five days were spent in rescue work before all the bodies were recovered.

The 'red alert' sounded at the Hoxton Community Centre at 66, New North Road — where there is a direct link with both Police and Fire Brigade headquarters — at 9.40 a.m., and within minutes a team of four, headed by Captain J. H. Burlison, with first-aid equipment, food and drink, was passing through the police cordon which encircled the station. Fire Brigade personnel helped to carry the party's gear down to platform nine where a rescue post was set up. Not for another two hours was a solitary press representative allowed to descend to the platform on behalf of the pressmen waiting at the surface.

To add to the general discomfort the temperature below quickly rose to over 100°. The team members had to strip to be able to continue working. A layer of dust and dirt covered a scene which looked like a shot from a film of a bomb incident in war time London. The Army team were soon called on for mortuary duty. Surgical gloves, plastic boots and a disinfectant trough were the order of the day. Carbon dioxide was building up and, until an air intake fan had been installed, members of the team had to take turns in coming to street level for rest and fresh air. Throughout the whole of the day — and until the last day of the rescue operation — meals were served at platform level to the police and firemen on duty. Any and every call upon the team was answered without delay. Officers accompanied the less seriously injured to hospital. Others visited the homes of those who had lost their lives and sought to bring Christian comfort. The coaches themselves were so impacted that it took two days' hard work to reach the main section of the front coach. Even then access was by narrow openings which firemen had cut through the twisted wreckage. In this way Captain Burlison crawled through the tangled metal to aid the medical staff operating on those who could not be moved until a foot or a hand had been amputated.

On March 19th, 1975, St. Paul's Cathedral was crowded for a memorial service, and on March 26th, 1975 Captain Burlison was one of the group of rescue workers received by the Prime Minister at 10, Downing Street. 'We took it for granted,' he was told, 'that you would be there.'

William Booth would not just have turned contentedly in his grave at such a word. His living spirit would have rejoiced greatly.

Bibliography

William Booth, Harold Begbie (Macmillan)

God's Soldier, St. John Ervine (Heinemann)

The General Next To God, Richard Collier (Fontana)

The Young William Booth, Bernard Watson (Max Parrish)

In Darkest England and The Way Out, William Booth (Charles Knight & Co.)

The Life of Mrs. Booth, Booth-Tucker (S.A.)

Catherine Booth, Catherine Bramwell-Booth (Hodder and Stoughton)

Mrs. Booth, W. T. Stead (Nisbet)

Popular Christianity, Catherine Booth (S.A.)

The Salvation Army in Relation to the Church and State, Catherine Booth (S.A.)

Bramwell Booth, Catherine Bramwell-Booth (Rich and Cowan)

Social Reparation, Living Epistles, Echoes and Memories, Bramwell Booth (all S.A.)

These Fifty Years, Bramwell Booth (Cassell)

The History of The Salvation Army, vol. 3, Sandall (Nelson)

An Outline History of The Salvation Army in New Zealand, Cyril Bradwell (typescript)

A History of The Salvation Army in New Zealand, 1883–1929, John C. Waite (typescript)

Salvation Chariot, Percival Dale (S.A.)

Notable Officers of The Salvation Army, Minnie Carpenter (S.A.)

Maiden Tribute, Madge Unsworth (S.A.)

Muktifauj, Booth-Tucker (S.A.)

Hotchpotch, Adelaide Cox (S.A.)

The Darkest England Gazette, 1893–1894

The Social Gazette, 1895–1916

The Deliverer

The Salvation Army Year Book

Orders & Regulations for Social Officers of The Salvation Army, 1898

Report of The Committee of Inquiry Upon The 'Darkest England' Scheme, Henry James and others (Harrison & Sons)

Sketches of The Salvation Army Social Work, G. R. Sims and others (S.A.)

Social Diseases and Worse Remedies, T. H. Huxley (Macmillan)

Churches and the Working Classes in Victorian England, K. S. Inglis (Routledge and Kegan Paul)

Patterns of Sectarianism, Bryan Wilson (Heinemann)

A Sociological Year Book of Religion, 5 (S.C.M.)

Marx & Engels on Religion (Progress Publishers)

Frank Smith, M.P., E. I. Champness (Whitefriars Press)

Devil's Island, Brian Peachment (Religious Education Press)

Into Unknown England, Peter Keating (Fontana)

Field Wing Bail Hostel, Home Office Research Studies, No. 30

The Darkest England Match Industry, D. C. Mitchell (privately printed)

Index

189